A GUIDE TO
Historic
BURIAL GROUNDS
IN NEWPORT

A GUIDE TO
Historic
BURIAL GROUNDS
IN NEWPORT

Lewis Keen

THE
History
PRESS

Published by The History Press
Charleston, SC
www.historypress.com

Front cover (counterclockwise from top right): Alfred Smith lot in Island Cemetery, Trinity Churchyard, Colonial Jewish Burial site entrance, Pompey Brenton stone detail, Common Burying Ground slate stones. *Photos by the author*.
Back cover, inset: Ida Lewis stone. *Photo by Barbara Austin*; *bottom*: Common Burying Ground map.

First published 2021

Manufactured in the United States

ISBN 9781467150163

Library of Congress Control Number: 2021938535

CONTENTS

CONTENTS

PREFACE

This work is intended to be a guide or primer for people interested in Newport's historic burial sites and colonial gravestones. Hopefully the guide will inspire the reader to seek additional information and does not assume the reader has a vast knowledge of the topics presented or an interest in excessively detailed information about each subtopic. With that in mind, excessive footnotes to verify facts or explore details within the publication have not been included. The bibliography may be useful for further research by those interested in continuing their exploration.

ACKNOWLEDGEMENTS

*I*t has been said that none of us is as smart as all of us, and writing this book supports this sentiment. Trudy Keen and Mary Jo Valdes provided much-needed assistance in reviewing the document to make it more worthy of publication. Trudy has impeccable written language skills and a talent for the efficient, clear communication of ideas. Her involvement in and support of the project are greatly appreciated. Mary Jo has a vast knowledge of Newport history and a sharp eye for spotting errors in fact or format. Her confirmation of the content and appreciation for the work were welcomed.

This publication would not have been possible without the work of many individuals whose previous efforts documented or preserved historic sites and stones in Newport. When the Common Burying Ground was at its worst, Edwin Connelly initiated the effort to improve the site and document its importance. Keith and Theresa Stokes kept a watchful eye on God's Little Acre for decades, and their research, presentations and website promoted the importance of it in American history. Ron Onorato, James Garman and John Canham undertook the installation of gravestones previously dislodged from their home locations. Vincent Luti's 2002 publication, *Mallet and Chisel*, provides a remarkable reference for anyone interested in the work of the Stevens carvers. In 2009, John Sterling, Barbara Austin and Letty Champion documented every colonial Newport gravestone and site. Their work about eighteenth-century burials, *Newport, Rhode Island Colonial Burial Grounds*, is the most comprehensive document ever created on the subject.

ACKNOWLEDGEMENTS

Many, but not all, burial sites in Newport are owned by the city. Its interest and support have been extremely important. Under the direction of Scott Wheeler, decades of neglect have been overcome, and burial sites and stones continue to be enhanced. The recent support of the city council and the rejuvenation of the Historic Cemetery Advisory Commission have reenergized the movement to preserve and promote burial sites and stones. The commission has been fortunate to have community volunteers of diverse talent and unwavering commitment serve on the commission.

Introduction

Colonial burying grounds and gravestones in Newport, Rhode Island, are remarkable. The sites reflect the society in which they were created, and the stones are historic documents as well as artistic treasures. As elsewhere in Rhode Island, many early inhabitants of Newport buried their loved ones in plots on family property. As Newport grew into a major colonial city, the leaders realized the city needed a substantial burial site; thus, the Common Burying Ground was established in 1665. By the time its sea of slate stones was complete, more than 85 percent of all seventeenth- and eighteenth-century burials for Newporters were located within its borders.[1] Reflective of Rhode Island's ideology, anyone could be buried in the site regardless of religion, economic status or ethnicity. No known Catholics are buried in the Common Burying Ground, as there were none in the city in that era, and colonial Jewish burials took place in a separate site as required by Jewish law. By the time of the American Revolution, Newport was home to nine religious congregations. As unique as each religion was in life, in death their members used the same gravestone designs, the same carvers and virtually the same burial practices.

The most significant section of the Common Burying Ground is the northern end, referred to as God's Little Acre. It includes the largest collection of gravestones for colonial (pre-1800) people of African heritage in the country. The limited documentation of the colonial African and early

1. John E. Sterling, et al., *Newport, Rhode Island Colonial Burial Grounds* (Hope: Rhode Island Genealogical Society, Special Publication No. 10, 2009), xvii.

Slate gravestones located in the Common Burying Ground. *Photo by the author.*

African American experience makes this site one of the most important extant sources for research.

In addition to the Common Burying Ground, Newport is fortunate to have numerous historic burial sites. They enhance the city's standing as a major repository of historic gravestones. Buried alongside governors of Rhode Island and family members of Roger Williams are individuals who helped create the city, the state and the nation.

The practice of using carved stone to mark graves began in the latter seventeenth century. In the early years, professionally carved stones displayed the work of prominent Boston carvers, but after 1705, Newport was home to its first known resident carver, John Stevens. His work can be seen in graveyards in the city and the surrounding region, but his true gift was establishing a stonecarving shop and tradition that continued for six generations. In 1926, that shop and those traditions passed into the hands of the Benson family and continues today.

Our burying grounds are places to remember the people who preceded us in life, learn about the history of the city and its people and experience one of America's earliest art forms. The time has come for our generation to undertake the responsibility to do what we can to preserve the stones and the sites for future generations.

Part I

COLONIAL BURIAL PRACTICES AND BURIAL SITES

State ID #	Site Name
NT001	Island Cemetery
NT002	Island Annex Cemetery
NT003	Common Burial Ground
NT004	Braman Cemetery
NT005	Old City Cemetery (North Cemetery)
NT006	St Mary's Cemetery
NT007	John Clarke Burial Ground
NT008	Friends Burial Ground
NT009	Coddington Burial Ground
NT010	Trinity Church Yard
NT011	Gov. Benedict Arnold Graveyard
NT012	United Congregational Churchyard
NT013	Colonial Jewish Burying Ground
NT014	Clifton Burial Ground
NT016	Coggeshall Burial Ground
NT019	St. Joseph's Old Catholic Cemetery
NT020	Judge Anthony Wilbur Lot

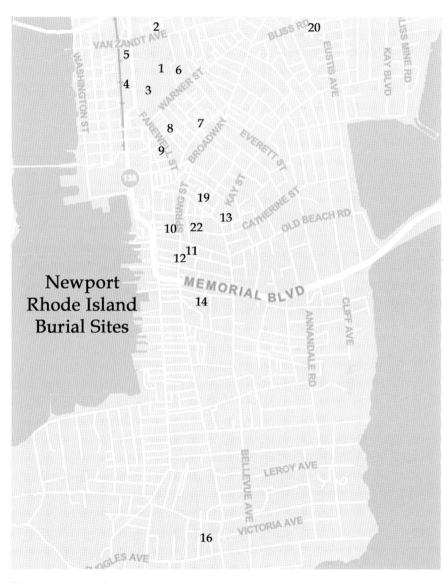

The numbers used for each burial site are consistent with numbers assigned by the State of Rhode Island, listed opposite. *Photo by the author.*

1

COLONIAL NEW ENGLAND
BURIAL PRACTICES

A major reason English families immigrated to North America was a desire for religious freedom. There were Christians who felt the Church of England had not correctly separated from the Catholic Church, and they sought to purify or reform Christianity. Once here, the Congregational Church became the only sanctioned religion throughout New England, a situation that prompted the formation of the Colony of Rhode Island in 1638. Here, Baptists, Quakers, Moravians, Congregationalists, Anglicans and Jews coexisted. While there were many religious tenets the groups disagreed on, in death their practices were almost identical.

The Christian sects all used the same gravestone designs and oriented the bodies in the same direction. Heads were west of the feet so that on Judgement Day the person could sit up to face the rising sun. This practice was not used by members of Jewish congregations. Devout Quakers did follow this practice but varied from the common practice of burying family members together.

The earliest professionally carved gravestones featured winged death's heads in the rounded middle section of the stone. The grim image illustrates the attitude that life had ended. Early stones may also be embellished with gourds and fruit along the side panels, believed to have religious meaning. Just as the seeds inside gourds produce new life once the casing is no more,

Above: Death heads were early imagery (iconography) used on gravestones. They can be found on gravestones throughout New England. *Photo by Barbara Austin; RI Historic Cemeteries website (RIHC).*

Opposite, top: Gourds used on gravestones were carved along the side panels. *RIHC composition by the author.*

Opposite, bottom: Soul effigies in a variety of styles became popular on gravestones in the eighteenth century. *Photo by the author.*

the soul would be reborn after the body died. As Puritan religious beliefs softened, so did imagery on gravestones, and death's heads were replaced with winged soul effigies. This change in image suggests the soul was going to a better place and is more reflective of the person than of the dead body. Some have suggested this image change was related to the Great Awakening of the 1740s, which emphasized the idea of salvation. Vines replaced gourds on the side panels, but the general design of the stones remained unchanged.

Organized religion in the early days of Rhode Island was minimally involved in burials and funerals. Churches may have rung bells to announce a death or funeral and perhaps a sermon was delivered weeks after the burial, but the movement of the reform congregations away from the Catholic Church and the Church of England was meant to reduce church involvement in burials. As a result, most burials were not in land adjacent to a house of worship. Family burial sites were the norm in Rhode Island, and in Newport, the Common Burying Ground served an important need for the community.

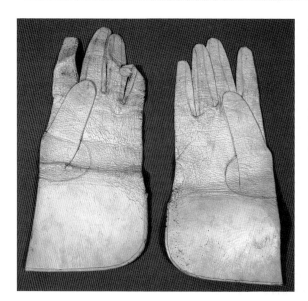

Above: Vines replaced gourds on side panels and exhibit a great deal of variety in design. *RIHC composition by the author.*

Left: Invitations to funerals were issued in the form of a pair of gloves. *Photo from historicipswich.org.*

Mourning rings were presented to close relatives and persons of note in the community. *Photo from historicipswich.org.*

Invitations to attend funerals were issued by the family often in the form of a pair of white gloves. Family members and close friends of the deceased may have also received mourning rings, gold bands decorated with death-related images. The body in the coffin was carried on a stand (bier) and covered with a cloth (pall) to the burial site. The funeral procession included sets of pallbearers carrying the coffin followed by the mourners. The grave was most often dug by friends of the deceased. Following the burial, friends and family often returned to the home of the deceased to share food and drink. The cost of funerals became so extreme in the eighteenth century that in 1741, Massachusetts passed a law limiting the amount of money spent on items like rings and gloves.[2]

2. Historic Ipswich, "Colonial New England Funerals," https://historicipswich.org/2019/10/12/colonial-new-england-funerals/.

2

BURIAL SITES

Burying grounds, *burial grounds*, *boneyards* and *graveyards* were commonly used terms in colonial New England as final resting places for the dead. These sites were not planned or designed but expanded organically as burials took place. The earliest burials may have been marked with wooden markers, but many were never marked at all. Stone replaced wood as a more long-lasting material to mark grave sites, and the earliest were fieldstones, some with information about the deceased etched into their surfaces. In the last part of the seventeenth century, the use of professionally carved headstones and footstones became the common practice to mark graves and dominated burial sites for the next one hundred years. Box tombs, table tombs and ledger stones were used concurrently throughout the region. While most graveyards were located on family-owned land, public sites and sites related to religious organizations were also established.

The term *cemetery* was introduced to New England in 1831 with the establishment of the Mount Auburn Cemetery outside of Boston, Massachusetts. Rural or garden cemeteries like Mount Auburn were founded in many communities in the country and were a clear departure from the graveyards. Cemeteries were designed by landscape architects to include not only the deceased, but also walkways, statuary and scenic vistas in an overall park-like environment. Unlike their predecessors that were often located in the heart of densely built-up urban areas, garden cemeteries were often built in less developed locations that were easily reached, usually on the edge of a city. In 1836, the City of Newport established it first cemetery, which soon became a private undertaking known as the Island Cemetery. About 1865, the city established the second cemetery, Old City Cemetery

Newport has more than twenty known burial sites. Some are surrounded by stone walls built in the 1800s to enclose stones predominantly from the 1700s. *Photo by the author.*

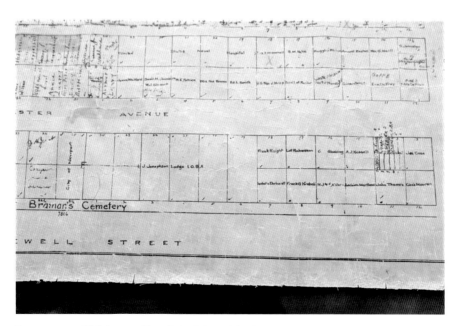

Braman map. This is a small section of the original map for the Braman Cemetery. The map is located in the vault at Newport City Hall and can be viewed at the City Clerk's Office. *Photo by the author.*

or North Common Burying Ground. The third site, Braman Cemetery, was established in 1898. Most cemeteries were established as for-profit businesses, but public and religious sites were also created.

Over the years, ownership of some cemeteries and burial grounds has changed. Some, like the Newport Common Burying Ground, were created as publicly owned sites and continue to operate that way today. Some sites, originally created as private entities, are no longer maintained by their original owners. The life expectancy of some families, religious institutions and corporations falls short of the life of the site. Once abandoned, these sites become either public domain or uncared-for orphans left to deteriorate.

One challenge in creating this publication was the inclusion of notable graves or burials for each site. Brief highlights of selected individuals are presented with the thought that if a reader's interest in a person is piqued, the reader could undertake further independent research. More problematic was the selection of the people to include. Recorded history tends to favor white males of the dominant religious group who were soldiers, politicians and religious leaders. Newport's history is dominated by these men, and while they are deserving of recognition, additional people have been included in this text to enrich the recorded history of the city.

Newport's colonial burial sites were most recently documented by John Sterling and his team. The information was published in 2009 and posted and updated on a statewide database. The information for each site is shared in the appendix, and additional information about the work can be found on pages 107–8.

BURIAL SITES INCLUDED IN THIS SECTION

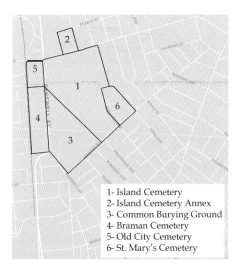

1- Island Cemetery
2- Island Cemetery Annex
3- Common Burying Ground
4- Braman Cemetery
5- Old City Cemetery
6- St. Mary's Cemetery

A detailed view of the cluster of burial sites located in the Farewell Street–Warner Street area. *Photo by the author.*

3

COMMON BURYING GROUND
AND GOD'S LITTLE ACRE

With a deep, sheltered harbor, Newport quickly became a thriving seaport and the largest city in the colony. In 1665, Dr. John Clarke donated about ten acres of his land for use as a burial site. Located on Farewell Street, the site contains more than 85 percent of Newport's colonial burials[3] and welcomed people of all faiths. With no known Catholics in the city and a separate Jewish burial site, as required by Jewish law, the Common Burying Ground welcomed Baptists, Quakers, Moravians, Anglicans, Congregationalists and people with no congregational affiliation. Politicians, soldiers, merchants, ship captains and seamen rest in this site. In addition to free Englishmen and women, others from around the world share the land. The first burial on the site was in 1666 for members of the Cranston family,[4] and the most recent burials date to the late twentieth century.

While burials continued on this site for more than three hundred years, its seventeenth- and eighteenth-century slate memorials are art treasures that enhance the historic fabric of the city. Some stones were created by master carvers located in the Boston area like William Mumford and Nathaniel Emmes, but the core of the collection represents the work of the Stevens shop established in Newport in 1705.

Among the many notable burials in this site is William Ellery (1727–1820), one of two Rhode Island signers of the Declaration of Independence

---

3. Sterling, Newport, *Rhode Island Colonial Burial Grounds*, xvii.
4. Ibid., 1.

This page, top: Newport's Common Burying Ground covers more than ten acres and includes about eight thousand graves. *Photo by the author.*

This page, bottom: This stone for Mary Cranston, who died in 1666, is the first known burial in the site. *Photo by Barbara Austin, RIHC.*

Opposite: Harte (died 1660) and John Garde (died 1665) were originally buried in another location and moved here before 1800. These are the oldest stones on the site. *Photos by Barbara Austin; RIHC composition by the author.*

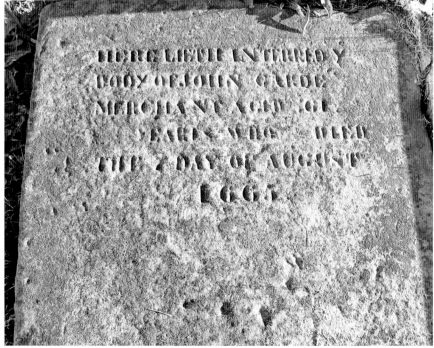

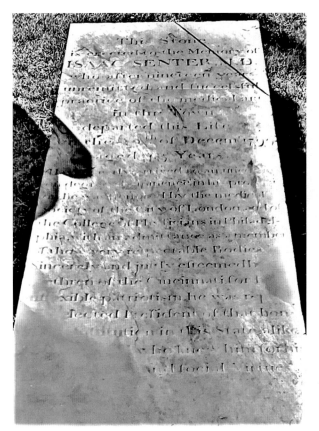

The stone for Dr. Isaac Senter (1754–1799) was preserved in 2020. The brick box was reconstructed and a missing corner on the slate ledger stone reconstructed. *Photo by the author.*

(map no. 4). He is joined by numerous politicians who served at every level of the government. Numerous veterans of every major war rest in this ground, including more than sixty men who served in the Revolutionary War. Perhaps the most notable, Dr. Isaac Senter (1754–1799), served under Benedict Arnold in the Battle of Quebec. Captured along with many other soldiers, Senter treated imprisoned Americans in Quebec and, after his return to Newport, enjoyed a career as a respected physician.

Ida Lewis (1842–1911) is perhaps the most famous woman buried on the site (map no. 10). She became the highest-paid lighthouse keeper in the country during her thirty-nine years on Lime Rock. Lewis is officially credited with saving eighteen lives in Newport Harbor, but thirty-six may be a more accurate number. People flocked to Newport to meet Lewis, and her most well-known admirers included Elizabeth Cady Stanton, Susan B. Anthony and President Ulysses Grant. Ann Franklin (1696–1763), America's first female printer, is also buried here (map no. 6). Wife of

Left: Ida Lewis gravestone. *Photo by Barbara Austin, RIHC.*

Below: God's Little Acre is the north part of the Common Burying Ground and is bordered by Farewell Street, Dyre Avenue and the Island Cemetery. *Photo by the author.*

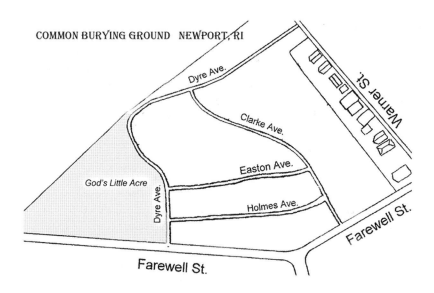

Above: The name *Cudjo* is an example of the African tradition of naming based on the day of the week of the birth. Cudjo was used for boys born on Monday. *Photo by Barbara Austin, RIHC.*

Opposite: *Quammine* was a name used by Africans for boys born on a Saturday. *Photo by Barbara Austin, RIHC.*

James Franklin, printer and older brother of Benjamin Franklin, Ann Franklin was active in the business with her husband and conducted it after his death.

The most notable section of the Common Burying Ground is the northern triangle referred to as God's Little Acre, the largest burial site with carved gravestones for colonial Africans in the country. According to Glen Knoblock, there are more monuments in this section for people of African heritage than in the rest of New England combined.[5] Although the total number of individuals buried here is unknown, there were at one time approximately 275 professionally carved slate headstones.

While the size of the collection is remarkable, each stone is an important historic and artistic artifact. The information, the images and the grouping of the stones inform us about not only the people for whom they were

5. Glenn Knoblock, *African American Historic Burial Grounds and Gravesites of New England* (Jefferson, NC: McFarland and Company, 2016), 170.

carved but also the society in which they lived. The majority of gravestones in God's Little Acre reflect the same artistry as the stones cut for European graves and are virtually identical to those stones. Their unique qualities include some wording that may state the person's enslaver, include names that reflect African heritage and provide information not documented in other records of the time. Toward the end of the eighteenth century, some stones display a revised image considered by some to show more African than European features. It's possible these images reflect the artistic design of the carver, John Stevens III, and were not intended to be a portrayal of African features. It is also possible Stevens was carving a more realistic representation of the deceased.

The stones located in God's Little Acre, in concert with existing documents of the time, provide an important resource for researchers today interested in interpreting the African experience in colonial America.

Stones considered to exhibit African features were carved by John Stevens III. *Photo by the author.*

This stone is signed as being carved by Pompe Stevens. His style is the same as William Stevens, and Pompe likely cut more stones than he is given credit for carving. *Photo by the author.*

Two important stones in God's Little Acre are for Cuffe Gibbs (1728–1768) and Pompey Lyndon (circa 1763–1765). Both stones are believed to have been carved by Pompe Stevens, an African enslaved by William Stevens. The Gibbs stone (map no. 8) is inscribed, "This stone was cut by Pompe Stevens in memory of his brother Cuffe Gibbs." Pompe Stevens's style of carving matches that of William Stevens, who likely trained him, suggesting that some stones currently attributed to William Stevens may have been carved by Pompe Stevens. Additionally, Pompey Lyndon was the child of Caesar Lyndon, who assisted Governor Josiah Lyndon in the affairs of the colony. Caesar Lyndon's diary is an important primary source for anyone researching the African experience in colonial New England. The most comprehensive interpretation of God's Little Acre can be found on the website maintained by the 1696 Heritage Group, www.colonialcemetery.com.

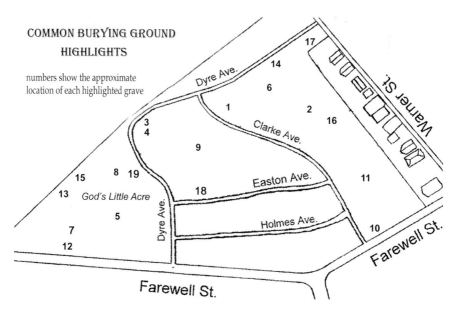

The highlights list and map are based on a self-guided walking tour developed by the Newport Historic Cemetery Advisory Commission in 2017. *Photo by the author.*

Notable Burials
in the Common Burying Ground

This list is based on a self-guided walking tour developed by the Newport Historic Cemetery Advisory Commission in 2017. Locations on the map are approximate.

Charles Bardin (1700–1773) was a member of Trinity Church and served the congregation, at times, as organist. His gravestone, carved by John Bull, was considered controversial for its depiction of Moses or possibly God. Biblical images on stones were extremely rare in colonial New England (map no. 1).

Samuel Cranston (1659–1727) was the longest-serving governor of Rhode Island (about thirty years). The legend is he was captured by pirates and missing for years before returning the day his wife was set to remarry. Cranston, Rhode Island, was named for Samuel Cranston (map no. 2).

Charles Dyre (1650–1709) was the son of Mary Dyre, a Quaker hanged in Boston for her religious beliefs in 1660. The Dyres were one of the original families to settle Newport and had land near the Navy hospital. The graves were moved here in 1889 due to development of the land that had been the family farm (map no. 3).

Arthur Flagg (1733–1810), also known as Arthur Tikey, was a member of the Seventh Day Baptist Church, a rope maker and a prominent member of the Free African Union Society. The use of the surname given to him after he arrived in Newport (Flagg) and his African name (Tikey) has been a subject of historical discussions (map no. 5).

James (1697–1735) and Ann Franklin (1696–1763). James Franklin was the first official printer for the colony of Rhode Island and the brother of Benjamin Franklin. After his death, his wife, Ann, became the official printer for the colony and the first female printer in the colonies. The family started publishing the *Newport Mercury* in 1758. The original press is located in the museum of the Newport Historical Society (map no. 6).

Newport Gardner family. Silva (circa 1783–1784), Charles Quamine (1794–1798), Abraham (circa 1796–1798) and Limas (?–1821) are buried together without the family patriarch. Newport Gardner, also known as Occramer Marycoo, was a member of the First Congregational Church, a musician, teacher and a founding member of the Free African Union Society in 1780. He died a free man in 1896 in Africa, where he is buried (map no. 7).

Langley children who died in infancy are memorialized with this six-foot-long gravestone carved by John Bull. Each effigy is virtually identical

Left: The stone for Ann Franklin, one of the first female printers in America. She ran the business after her husband, James, died. *Photo by Barbara Austin, RIHC.*

Below: A six-foot-long stone carved for deceased children of the Langley family by John Bull. *Photo by the author.*

and hand-carved. The children—Sarah, Sarah, Nathaniel, Royal, William and William—died between 1771 and 1785 (map no. 9).

SOPHIA LITTLE (1799–1893) was an author and social reformer. Little was active in the antislavery movement and the rehabilitation of prisoners released from jail (map no. 18).

DUCHESS QUAMINO (1739–1804) was active in the African Union Society and influential in the life of William Ellery Channing, foremost minister

Dr. Rice is buried here with family members. Her brother Dr. George Rice graduated from Dartmouth College and practiced medicine in England, where he worked with Dr. Joseph Lister. *Photo by the author*.

in the Unitarian Church. Her baking skills led her to be called the "Pastry Queen of Rhode Island," and George Washington enjoyed her frosted plum cakes on at least two occasions (map no. 12).

DR. HARRIET RICE (1866–1958) was educated in Newport public schools and the first African American graduate of Wellesley College. In 1919, the French government awarded her the Bronze Medal of Reconnaissance for her efforts in treating those injured in World War I (map no. 19).

JOHN STEVENS (circa 1647–1736) arrived in Newport in 1705 and founded a masonry and gravestone carving business. Six generations of Stevenses carved gravestones (map no. 14).

JANE STUART (1812–1888) was an accomplished artist and daughter of Gilbert Stuart (1755–1828), colonial America's foremost portrait painter. Trained by her father, Jane Stuart assisted with many of his portraits when his health failed. She was able to support herself and family members with her talents and was a lively member of Newport society (map no. 16).

WILLIAM VERNON (circa 1720–1806) was instrumental in the formation of the colonial Navy, and his house in Newport was Rochambeau's headquarters during the American Revolution. It was in this house that Rochambeau and General George Washington made plans that led to the Battle of Yorktown (map no. 17).

GUIDED TOURS OF THE Common Burying Ground are often offered by the Newport Historical Society, and tours of God's Little Acre are often provided by the Rhode Island Black Heritage Society.

4

FAMILY SITES

Clifton/Golden Hill, Coddington/Governors, John Clarke, Coggeshall, Arnold, Wilbur

CLIFTON OR GOLDEN HILL BURIAL GROUND AND THE WANTON VAULT

Located on Golden Hill Road behind the Newport Public Library, this burial site was originally owned by Thomas Clifton and may have served as a family plot. Quaker death records indicate Thomas Clifton died in 1681, but there is no known gravestone for him or any indication where he is buried. About 1675, the site was being used by members of the Society of Friends. Despite the Quaker norm for undecorated stones, there are 160 exceptional examples of stones, many from important colonial carvers.

A private family burial site for the Wanton family was located on the east end of the Clifton land about 1771. The two sites combine to appear as one today. The Wanton section contains the only known colonial-era crypt for burials in the city and is marked by a marble stone cap.

NOTABLE BURIALS IN THIS SITE INCLUDE

GOVERNOR JEREMY CLARKE (1605–1651) was one of the men who founded Newport in 1639. He served as assistant to Governor William Coddington and assumed the governor's responsibilities when Coddington stepped down from the position.

The Clifton Burial Ground is also known as the Golden Hill Burial Ground. *Photo by the author.*

This marble cap marks the entrance to the Wanton crypt. *Photo by the author.*

Mother and daughter share a stone carved by John Stevens I. *Photo by Barbara Austin, RIHC.*

GOVERNOR WALTER CLARKE (circa 1637–1714) served as governor, was the son of Governor Jeremy Clarke and married Roger Williams's daughter Freeborn.

GOVERNOR JOSEPH WANTON (1705–1780) served as governor during the *Gaspee* Affair and did not help the Crown bring those responsible to justice. Despite his apparent support of the perpetrators of the burning of the *Gaspee*, his actions closer to 1776 were interpreted as Loyalist and prompted his removal from office.

GOVERNOR WILLIAM WANTON (1670–1733) was related to three other members of the Wanton family who served as governors. He served as governor from 1732 to 1733.

MARY CRANSTON (circa 1663–1710) was the wife of Governor Samuel Cranston, who served as governor longer than any person in Rhode Island history. Legend states that Mary was set to remarry after Samuel (noted in the Common Burying Ground highlights) had been missing for years, when he returned to Newport on the day the marriage was to take place.

FREEBORN CLARKE (circa 1635–1710) was the daughter of Roger Williams and wife of Governor Walter Clarke.

JOB TOWNSEND (circa 1699–1765) was the founding member of the famous Townsend and Goddard furniture makers.

CODDINGTON/GOVERNORS BURIAL GROUND

The Coddington or Governors Burying Ground is located on Farewell Street and North Baptist Street. William Coddington was the original English settler of this parcel and later placed it under the control of the Newport Quaker Meeting. Of the ninety-four burials known here, fifty-eight inscribed stones remain. Six colonial governors of Rhode Island are buried here:

NICHOLAS EASTON (1593–1675) served in many offices in addition to the governorship. As one of the founders of Newport, his name remains to this day at Easton's Beach and Easton Point.

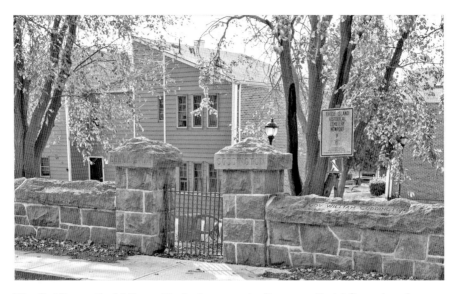

The Coddington Burial Ground is also known as the Governors Burial Ground, as six colonial Rhode Island governors are buried here. *Photo by the author.*

WILLIAM CODDINGTON (1601–1678) served as governor decades after creating early dissension in the colony. He was a founder of Newport in 1639.

WILLIAM CODDINGTON JR. (1651–1689) served as governor for two years, 1683 to 1685.

HENRY BULL (1610–1694) was an original settler of Newport and served as governor in 1685 and again in 1690. His family had an influence in the city for many generations.

JOHN EASTON (1624–1705) arrived in Newport with his father as a teenager in 1639 and, like his father, served as governor (1690–1695).

JOHN WANTON (1672–1740) served as governor the last six years of his life, 1734 to 1740.

JOHN CLARKE BURIAL GROUND

This site is located on Dr. Marcus Wheatland Boulevard and Callender Avenue. Dr. John Clarke was a founding member of the City of Newport and obtained the Rhode Island Royal Charter of 1663, granting religious freedom to residents of the colony. A Baptist minister, Clarke gave this land to his church to be used for burials. No marker for Clarke was established

This is the most recent memorial on the John Clarke Burial Ground site. *Photo by the author.*

when he died, but three have since been installed in his honor. He was a clergyman, physician and statesman. Additional burials on this site include Clarke's wives, other Baptist pastors and people connected with Reverend Michael Eddy, who died in 1834.

COGGESHALL BURIAL GROUND

This site contains fifty burials and thirty-six inscribed stones and is located on Coggeshall Avenue south of the Breakers Stable. The death date on the gravestone for John Coggeshall (died 1647) is the oldest in Rhode Island. The gate and wall around the site were added in 1854 by Russell Coggeshall. Notable burials here include:

JOHN COGGESHALL (circa 1591–1647) was the first president of the colony under the patent obtained by Roger Williams. It is believed that his gravestone carving was the inspiration for John Stevens's work beginning in 1705.

ABRAHAM REDWOOD (1709–1788) was the founder of the library that bears his name.

BENJAMIN ELLERY (1725–1797) was the brother of a signer of the Declaration of Independence and husband of Abraham Redwood's daughter.

The Coggeshall Burial Site features a wall erected by a descendant in 1854. *Photo by the author.*

John Coggeshall's gravestone is the oldest dated gravestone in Rhode Island. *Photo by Barbara Austin, RIHC.*

Grave of Abraham Redwood. *Photo by Barbara Austin, RIHC.*

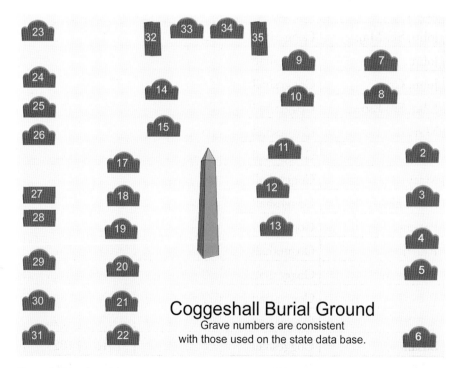

Coggeshall burial map. *Image by the author.*

		RI Grave #	Born	Died
Abraham	Coggeshall	19	1683	1758
Abraham	Coggeshall	25	1787c	1801
Arthur Sterry, Ds	Coggeshall	06	1873	1958
Benjamin	Coggeshall	08	1672c	1739
Comfort	Coggeshall	No stone	1691c	1725
Elisha	Coggeshall	30	1724c	1808
Elizabeth	Coggeshall	29	1728c	1803
Elizabeth	Coggeshall	14	1664c	1748
Elizabeth	Coggeshall	26	1750c	1830
Freegift	Coggeshall	15	1659c	1728
Hannah	Coggeshall	No stone	1721	1780
Henry	Coggeshall	31	1759c	1840
James	Coggeshall	No stone	1712c	1789
James	Coggeshall	02	1660c	1712
John, Sr., Maj.	Coggeshall	12	1619c	1708
John	Coggeshall	24	1747c	1747
John, Capt.	Coggeshall	28	1757c	1827
John, Sr., Esq.	Coggeshall	04	1591c	1647
Mary	Coggeshall	05	1595c	1684
Mary	Coggeshall	31	1767c	1851
Mary	Coggeshall	13	1649c	1731
Nathaniel	Coggeshall	10	1713c	1714
Patience	Coggeshall	18	1731c	1792
Patience	Coggeshall	11	1640c	1676
Rebeckah	Coggeshall	09	1704c	1714
Russell	Coggeshall	27	1788	1864
Sarah	Coggeshall	07	1689c	1726
Susanna	Coggeshall	28	1751c	1829
William	Cozzens	23	1779c	1801

Benjamin, Esq.	Ellery	35	1725c	1797
Mehetable	Ellery	35	1731c	1794
Edward	Hardman	03	1678c	1733
Elizabeth	Perrin	17	1711c	1794
Abraham, Esq.	Redwood	32	1710c	1788
Martha	Redwood	32	1709c	1760
Sarah	Redwood	33	1740c	1819
William	Redwood	34	1734c	1784
Catharine	Taylor	21	1756c	1847
Coggeshall	Taylor	22	1784	1811
Nicholas, Esq.	Taylor	21	1754c	1829
Patience	Taylor	20	1783c	1848

GOVERNOR BENEDICT ARNOLD GRAVEYARD

Located on Pelham Street between Spring Street and Bellevue Avenue, this site was established by Governor Benedict Arnold (1615–1678) for his family and his relatives in 1675. His great-grandson, of the same name, was a general in the Revolutionary War who is best remembered as a traitor to the country. After the Revolution, the property was inherited by Arnold descendants and the site sold. There are fifty-three gravestones on this site today, but thirteen other original stones are no longer here. It is remarkable that any stones exist, as the entire site was lost for nearly ninety years when a house was built on-site around 1900 and all the stones buried under a

The burial site of Governor Benedict Arnold is located on Pelham Street. *Photo by the author.*

46

"cottage." Alice Brayton purchased the property in 1946 and, with the help of John Howard Benson and T.J. Brown, removed the cottage and restored the site to its current configuration. Her publication *The Burying Place of Governor Arnold* (1960) is a wonderful document of the site, which was later given to the Preservation Society of Newport County.

Notable Burials

GOVERNOR BENEDICT ARNOLD (1615–1678) served numerous times as president and governor of the colony and was also a wealthy man. His estate stretched from Thames Street to current-day Bellevue Avenue and included his stone-built mill, known today as the Newport Tower.

WILBUR

The Judge Anthony Wilbur site is located near the intersection of Bliss Road and Eustis Avenue. It contains twenty-seven burials of the Ensworth, Hazard, Peckham and Wilbur families. Vegetation overgrowth was removed from the site and five marble stones conserved in 2018 by the city.

Judge Anthony Wilbur site is located near the intersection of Bliss Road and Eustis Avenue. *Photo by the author.*

5

RELIGIOUS SITES

Touro, Trinity, Quaker, Congregational, Moravian, St. Joseph's, St. Mary's

TOURO OR COLONIAL JEWISH BURIAL GROUND

Located at the intersection of Bellevue Avenue, Kay Street and Touro Street across from the Hotel Viking sits the oldest surviving Jewish burial ground in the country. It was established in 1677 and expanded in 1768 to serve the Jewish community that arrived around 1658. The majority of the congregation originated in Spain and Portugal, and many spent years in Amsterdam or the Caribbean before arriving in Newport.

The oldest stone dates to 1761 and the newest from 1866. The stone design is identical to stones carved for Christians with one notable difference. In addition to English, Hebrew, Ladino, Spanish, Portuguese and Latin can be found on stones for colonial Jewish Newporters. In 1843, the Egyptian Revival gate and fencing designed by Isaiah Rogers were added to the site.

Longfellow visited the site on July 9, 1852, and was inspired to write a poem about the burial ground, as was Emma Lazarus in 1867.

Notable Burials

JUDAH TOURO (1775–1854) was the youngest son of Isaac Touro, who was the first spiritual leader of the Newport Jewish Congregation. Judah Touro was America's first great philanthropist, whose substantial donation helped

Above: Isaiah Rogers designed the entrance and gate around this site, which is similar to the one he designed for the Granary Burying Ground in 1840. The project was funded by Judah Touro. *Photo by the author.*

Right: While this stone exhibits the carver's style (William Stevens), the addition of Hebrew text sets apart this and some other Jewish colonial stones. *Photo by Barbara Austin, RIHC.*

fund the Bunker Hill Monument in Boston. He made his fortune as a merchant and shipper in New Orleans and in 1854 contributed $10,000 to the City of Newport to buy land that included a stone tower. While his gift was not enough for the purchase, when the city did acquire the property, it was named Touro Park in honor of Judah Touro's generosity. His monument in this burial site was designed by Isaiah Rogers, the architect he hired to design the gates and fencing.

Isaac Touro died and was buried in Jamaica, but his family, including his wife and children, are here and memorialized by these obelisks. *Photo by the author.*

Abraham Touro (1774–1822) was the oldest son of Rabbi Isaac Touro. who donated funds to pave the street between the synagogue and the burial site. This bequest is the reason the street was renamed Touro Street.

Moses Seixas (circa 1743–1809) wrote to President Washington in 1790, which prompted a response that confirmed the concept of religious freedom in America. These letters predated the inclusion of religious freedom in the First Amendment to the U.S. Constitution.

Trinity Churchyard

The churchyard at Trinity Church is the most quintessential English burial site in the city. This Anglican congregation was established in 1698, and the existing building, which dates from 1726, was enlarged in the 1760s. The oldest monument from 1704 for Thomas Mallett is among the 246 other graves marked with excellent examples of colonial-era carved stones. Many members of the congregation are buried in the Common Burying Ground, as burial on church property was reserved for prominent and

Trinity Churchyard. *Photo by the author.*

faithful members.[6] In addition to the burials around the church, the interior is enhanced by handsome stone monuments and stained-glass windows. John B. Hattendorf's publication *Semper Eadem: A History of Trinity Church in Newport 1698–2000* includes detailed information about the monuments in the church as well as the graves outside.

Notable Burials

Reverend James Honyman (1675–1750) first visited Newport as a Navy chaplain in 1701 and returned in 1704 to lead the congregation. His appointment was opposed by a faction of the congregation that supported another candidate, and a conflict continued until 1709, when Honyman was accepted as minister by a majority of the members. Honyman's decades of service to the church ended with his death in 1750. Under his guidance, the church was built in 1701 and a newer structure in 1728. No other clergy served Trinity as long as did Honyman.

6. Sterling, *Newport, Rhode Island Colonial Burial Grounds*, 362.

Francis Malbone (1727–1785) arrived in Newport from Virginia to join his uncle Godfrey in business. The Malbones made fortunes as privateers, merchants, slave traders and distillers. In 1758, Francis Malbone built a mansion on Thames Street that is attributed to Peter Harrison, one of America's first architects. In 1762, Malbone, along with three other members of Trinity, funded the expansion of the church to its current configuration. Francis Malbone was the eleventh-richest man in the city in 1772.

Nathaniel Kay (circa 1675–1734) served the City of Newport as the customs collector for the king of England. Active in the church vestry for many years, he left property and funds to Trinity when he died. He funded a school for poor boys that stood at the corner of School and Mary Streets. Gilbert Stuart, an important American artist, and Benjamin Waterhouse, who introduced the smallpox vaccine to America, were students at the school in their youth. The school was rebuilt in 1799 and in 1868 became the home of Shiloh Baptist Church. Kay Street and Kay Chapel in Newport are named for Nathaniel Kay.

Lucia Berkeley (1731) was the infant daughter of George Berkeley, known later as Bishop Berkeley. She died three days before the family planned to return to England and was buried alongside Nathaniel Kay. The Berkeleys' time in Newport (1729–1731) inspired the creation of the Redwood Library (1747). In 1733, Bishop Berkeley gifted an organ to the church.

Mary Brett Shaw Thurston (1740–1819) was appointed by Reverend Browne to conduct a school for enslaved children. The school soon had thirty students, half boys and half girls. In July 1763, Benjamin Franklin visited Trinity to inspect the progress of the school under the direction of Brett.

Dr. William Hunter (1731–1777) is credited with giving the first course of anatomical lectures in America. He died from a fever he caught while attending a British soldier during the American Revolution.

William Hunter Jr. (1774–1848) was the son of Dr. Hunter and educated in the law in England. He entered politics when he returned to Newport and served in state government and as a U.S. senator. He is most associated with a colonial-era house in Newport he owned from 1805 to 1849. The house was later purchased and restored by the Preservation Society of Newport County and is known today as the Hunter House.

Quaker or Friends Burial Ground

Unwelcomed in other New England colonies, the Society of Friends or Quakers arrived in Rhode Island, specifically Newport, in 1657. Their desire to break with the Church of England and Catholic practices was evident in that the earliest Quaker burials were in family plots or the Common Burying Ground and not connected to a house of worship. A Quaker burial site was later established near their meetinghouse, and its oldest stone dates to 1728. It is likely that earlier burials took place on this site, but either the graves were never marked or the stones were lost over time. Some burial sites in Newport that started as family sites later allowed fellow Quakers to use the site. The Clifton Burial site and the Coddington site are good examples of this practice. The burial practices of Quakers were unique in the dating of stones and the sequence of burials. Since the names of the months of

the year were believed to have pagan origins, they were not used on Quaker gravestones. A death on "November 10, 1817" would be carved as "11 mo. 10th, 1817" on a proper Quaker stone. The stone included the name of the person and possibly their age. Colonial Quakers were discouraged from using highly decorated stones, but this practice was ignored by many wealthy Quaker merchants. The practice of burying people sequentially by death date rather than in family units was another Quaker practice that was not followed by all members of the faith.

A Quaker gravestone displaying the use of a number rather than the name for the month. *Photo by the author.*

UNITED CONGREGATIONAL CHURCHYARD

Colonial Newport had two Congregational churches; the first was established in 1695 and the second in 1728. Burials of church members were not connected to land adjacent to the house of worship, and most congregants were buried in the Common Burying Ground. The land for the First Congregational Society that stood on Mill Street was given by Governor Benedict Arnold.[7] Behind the church were the graves of the Reverend Clap, the Reverend Helyer and the Reverend Hopkins. These graves were relocated to a lot on the side of the United Congregational Church located on Spring Street.

---

7. Alice Brayton, *The Burying Place of Governor Arnold* (Newport, RI: privately printed, 1960), 13.

First Congregational Church, Mill Street, 1729. By Cotton Palmer
of Taunton. As it appeared in 1740.
From Newell's lithograph.

The First Congregational Church on Mill Street as depicted by Downing and Scully in *The Architectural History of Newport, Rhode Island.*

St. Joseph's Cemetery

The first Catholic parish in Rhode Island, St. Joseph's, was established in 1828 by the Boston Diocese. The congregation met in a preexisting structure on Barney Street, and an adjacent burial site was quickly established. The burial site today is maintained by volunteers from the Newport Museum of Irish History.

St. Mary's Cemetery

St. Joseph's congregation grew and split, and in 1848, St. Mary's was established. A new church was built on Spring Street and current-day

Top: St. Joseph Catholic Church once stood alongside the burial site on Barney Street. *Photo by the author.*

Bottom: Saint Mary's Cemetery, located at Warner Street and Kingston Avenue in Newport. *Photo by the author.*

Memorial Boulevard, and burials did not take place near the church but in a separate lot east of the Island Cemetery. John Sterling states that by 1890 the site was filled, and Catholic burials continued at St. Columba's Roman Catholic Cemetery in Middletown.

6

OLD CITY CEMETERY (NORTH COMMON BURYING GROUND), BRAMAN CEMETERY, ISLAND CEMETERY

OLD CITY CEMETERY AND BRAMAN CEMETERY

The Old City Cemetery and the Braman Cemetery line the west side of Farewell Street. These two sites were independently created but now appear as one and were established to serve the city as the Common Burying Ground became filled and additional burial spaces were needed. The Old City Cemetery is also known as the North Common Burying Ground and was established about 1865. It has always been a city-owned site and contains about five hundred graves. The most notable grave is for ARTHUR BURTON (1897–1918), the only African American service member from Rhode Island to be killed in action during World War I.

The Braman Cemetery was incorporated on March 3, 1898, by David B. Braman, Daniel B. Braman and Robert N. Fell on family land that had been farmed by John C. Braman. The city assumed responsibility for the site when the cemetery was "forfeited" on September 30, 1980. Braman Cemetery was most active in the twentieth century and reflects the diversity of the city. The site contains approximately 2,500 burials and includes Jewish sections as well as sections for U.S. Navy–related burials.

Newport has had a connection to the U.S. Navy since colonial times. A "new" Navy hospital opened in 1910 and was expanded in 1918 to accommodate one thousand patients. The cemetery has two sections purchased by the hospital for those who died or were pronounced dead

Above: Braman Cemetery was established in 1898 on land farmed in earlier years by the Braman family. *Photo by the author.*

Left: Arthur Burton's grave is marked by a government-issued stone. *Photo by the author.*

there. Numerous other people who served in the military are buried throughout the site.

Members of Newport's twentieth-century African American community buried in Braman are located throughout the site. Servicemen, politicians, educators, businessmen and religious leaders were just some of the community members who contributed their efforts and talents to the city and the country.

Above: Symbols of faith appear on government-issued gravestones starting with World War I. Earlier stones feature information in a sunken shield. *Photo by the author.*

Left: While many Greek stones are found in Braman Cemetery, a number are also located in the God's Little Acre section of the Common Burying Ground. *Photo by the author.*

Opposite, top: Braman Cemetery includes three Jewish sections and additional individual Jewish grave sites. *Photo by the author.*

Opposite, bottom: This map of Braman Cemetery is based on the original map and shows notable burials. *Photo by the author.*

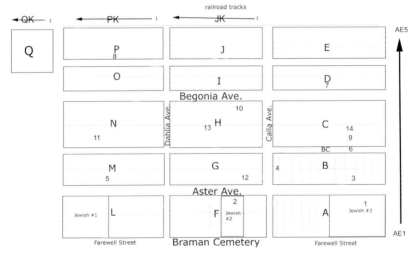

The numbers indicte an approximate location of the highlighted individuals for this site.

By 1896, there were four Greek residents in Newport; they came from the island of Skiathos and were later joined by others from Skiathos and Lesbos. Opportunities in the local fishing industry and tensions between Greece and Turkey may have encouraged people to move to Newport. The growing Newport Greek community was employed in a variety of jobs. Saint Spyridon's congregation (Greek Orthodox) was chartered in 1915 and worshipped at many places before buying its current house of worship on Thames Street in 1924. Greek burials are scattered throughout the Braman site.

Numerous Jewish groups and individuals purchased lots in Braman. The fenced-off sections, required by Jewish law, are noticeable features along Farewell Street. The various burials were brought together under the oversight of the newly chartered Jewish Cemetery Unification Association in 1976.

Notable Burials

RABBI DAVID BARUCH (1847–1899) was born in Amsterdam and living in New York City when he was hired (1894) to serve as spiritual leader at Touro Synagogue. He was the second rabbi to serve the congregation, which was reestablished in the 1880s (map no. 1).

RABBI JACOB BERNSTEIN (1885–1937) was one of the spiritual leaders of Newport's other Orthodox Jewish congregation, Ahavas Achim, which was in existence from 1915 to 1981. He was born in Russia and immigrated in 1901 (map no. 2).

DAVID BRAMAN (1845–1921) was one of the founders of the Braman Cemetery on land he helped his father farm. He was an active businessman in Newport and served on the boards of a number of banks (map no. 3).

DANIEL BURDICK BRAMAN (1850–1907) was one of the founders of the Braman Cemetery with his brother David. Daniel was an 1875 graduate of Brown University and, like his brother, served on a number of boards of Newport banks (map no. 4).

APOSTOLOS B. CASCAMBAS (1879–1950) arrived in New York City from Greece in 1892 and was a candy maker (confectioner). He became a naturalized citizen in 1912 and registered for the World War I and World War II drafts. He served as the first president of the local AHEPAN (American Hellenic Educational Progressive Association) chapter. His shop served soda with cream "right off the farm" for forty years at the corner of Long Wharf and Thames (map no. 5).

REVEREND DANIEL CHASE EASTON (1844–1907) died serving as a Baptist minister in Rockport, Massachusetts, but his burial in Newport speaks to his deep roots in the city. His ancestors included Governor Nicholas Easton, one of the founders of Newport, and Myles Standish, who arrived on the *Mayflower*. His son, Dr. Charles Daniel Easton, practiced medicine in Newport beginning in 1907 (map no. 6).

DR. SAMUEL G. ELBERT SR. (1865 or 1868–1939) was born in Maryland and was one of the first African American doctors in the state of Delaware.

Major Gaines is buried alongside family members. *Photo by the author.*

He earned his medical degree from Howard University and completed postgraduate coursework at the University of Pennsylvania. While living in Wilmington, Delaware, Dr. Elbert devoted much of his time to advance the education of youth in his community. ELLA SMITH ELBERT (1865–1955), wife of the doctor, was born in Newport and the sister of Dr. Daniel A. Smith (circa 1880–1971). It is likely the couple is buried in Newport because they moved here to be closer to her family (map no. 7).

GEORGE GAINES (1864–1951), ALBERT GAINES (1895–1951) and MAJOR WILLIAM JACKSON GAINES (1923–2012). George Gaines brought his family to Newport between 1910 and 1920. His sons, George, John and Albert, served in World War I. Albert Gaines later married and fathered six children. His son, William Gaines, graduated from Rogers High School in 1940 and worked in hotels, shining shoes to earn money to attend college. When World War II broke out, he was attending Virginia Union University in Richmond, Virginia, but left school to enlist in the Army. During his decades of service to the country, he saw active duty at Iwo Jima and Korea and was stationed in Europe during the Cold War years. He pioneered the design, development and implementation of a standard Army-wide automated munitions management and reporting system for which he was inducted into the U.S. Army Ordnance Corps Hall of Fame (1994), the first African American to be so honored. His brother PAUL GAINES (1932–2020) was the first African American mayor elected in Newport and New England (map no. 8).

Joseph J. Henry (1889–1908) died when his clothing was caught in gun turret gears, which snapped his neck, during training in Newport. He was a native of Memphis, Tennessee, and had joined the Navy the previous October. This impressive monument was funded by his shipmates on the USS *Mississippi* (map no. 9).

Armstead Hurley (1854–1932) arrived in Newport in 1886 from Culpepper County, Virginia, and became a successful house painter. He was a deacon and served as treasurer at Shiloh Baptist Church and was active politically in the local Republican Party. Hurley was also a member of the Odd Fellows Lodge and a Mason (map no. 10).

Reverend Louis Victor Jeffries (1881–1935) arrived in Newport to be the spiritual leader of Mt. Olivet Baptist Church from 1926 to 1935. Under his leadership, the church was raised, the Sunday School room enlarged and other facilities added to the building (map no. 11).

Martha Rebekah Goode Jeffries Calloway (1899–1968) married Reverend Jeffries in Virginia and arrived in Newport with him in 1926. She was in charge of the Vacation Bible School, a member and later president of the Newport Woman's Christian Temperance Union and presented lectures in the community. While her name is inscribed on the stone, she is not buried here. Following the death of her husband, she moved to Virginia to attend Virginia Union University, where she earned her diploma. Martha Jeffries went on to earn master's degrees from both Columbia and Andover Newton Theological Seminary. In addition to serving as dean of women at Virginia Union University, she was affiliated with Spelman College. In 1945, Martha Jeffries married Samuel Calloway and is buried with her parents and siblings in Woodland Cemetery in Richmond, Virginia (map no. 11).

Reverend Carl A.R. Liljewall (1886–1942) served as minister at the Calvary Methodist Church on Annandale Road, but his main congregation was in Providence, Rhode Island. He emigrated from Sweden in 1906 (map no. 12).

Nicholas G. Spiratos (1894–1967) was born in Cephalonia, Greece, immigrated in 1908 and served as president of St. Spyridon's Church from 1946 to 1948 and 1952 to 1953. A businessman, he was best known for Blue Moon Gardens, a club that served Navy personnel from 1933 to 1966 (map no. 13).

Axel Sundquist (1867–1910) was born in Finland and immigrated to the United States. He enlisted in the Navy in 1893, and while serving on the USS *Marblehead* during the Spanish-American War, he cleared twenty-seven contact mines from Guantanamo Bay. He was awarded the Medal of Honor for his bravery (map no. 14).

Axel Sundquist
has two
gravestones
located together.
Photo by the author.

The entrance to Island Cemetery on Warner Street. *Photo by the author.*

ISLAND CEMETERY AND ANNEX

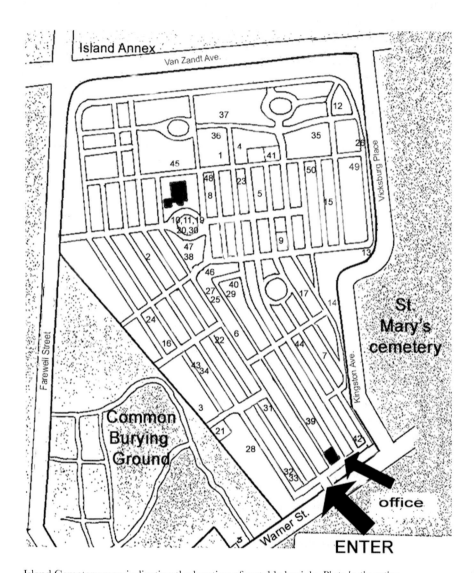

Island Cemetery map indicating the location of notable burials. *Photo by the author.*

In the early 1800s, burial practices started to change with the creation of the rural or garden cemetery. Following the establishment of Mount Auburn Cemetery in Cambridge, many cities adopted this concept for the final resting place of their inhabitants. The City of Newport purchased land northeast of the Common Burying Ground in 1836, and with the assistance of Henry Bull and William W. Freeborn, the city's garden cemetery was planned. In 1848, the site was sold to the plot owners who incorporated it under the name Island Cemetery Company. In 1851, the company added the adjacent Willow Cemetery to the site. This fashionable cemetery became the final resting place of many of Newport's most important people of the Gilded Age. Starting in 1886, the Belmont Memorial Chapel was constructed; about 1894, a receiving vault was built (no longer stands), and in 1902 an office building was constructed. The Island Cemetery Annex was added to the holdings in August 1926.

Notable Newport Burials

HUGH AUCHINCLOSS (1897–1976) was born at Hammersmith Farm in Newport and became a lawyer and stockbroker. In 1942, he married Janet Lee Bouvier, the mother of future first lady Jacqueline Bouvier Kennedy, whose marriage to Senator Kennedy took place in Newport (map no. 1).

GEORGE T. DOWNING (1819–1903) was a successful New York restaurateur prior to moving to Newport in 1848 to continue his career. He was important as a leader in the antislavery movement and the Underground Railroad and for lobbying Congress for equal rights for African Americans. When Downing died, the *Boston Globe* referred to him as the "foremost colored man in the country" (map no. 2).

MAJOR JOHN HANDY (1756–1828) read the Declaration of Independence on July 20, 1776, from the Colony House to the assembled citizens and reprised the reading fifty years later. When his land in Newport was later subdivided, the new streets were named for his sons: Levin, William, Thomas and John (map no. 3).

RICHARD MORRIS HUNT (1827–1895) was an important American architect and the first to graduate from the École des Beaux-Arts in Paris. His buildings defined nineteenth-century New York City, and his work includes the Biltmore Estate in Asheville, North Carolina, and the base of the Statue of Liberty. He designed more than forty buildings in Newport, including his best known, the Breakers Estate (map no. 4).

Left: George Downing was an important civil rights advocate. *Photo by the author.*

Right: Richard Morris Hunt's grave site is one of the most significant in the cemetery. *Photo by the author.*

The Smith family lot includes a monument designed by Augustus Saint Gaudins. *Photo by the author.*

EDWARD KING (1815–1875) earned a fortune in the China trade and, upon his return to Newport, invested in real estate in the city. He is acknowledged as the largest landowner in the history of Newport. At times he partnered with JOHN N.A. GRISWOLD (1822–1909) in purchasing properties. Both men had important houses built. The Edward King House (1845–47) is a classic Italianate Villa designed by Richard Upjohn, and the JNA Griswold House (1861–63) by Richard Morris Hunt on Bellevue Avenue is an early Stick-style building (map no. 5, 46).

HENRY LEDYARD (1812–1880) served as mayor of Detroit, Michigan. Later in life, he raised funds for and served as the first president of the Newport Hospital and also served as president of the Redwood Library (map no. 48).

GEORGE CHAMPLIN MASON (1820–1895), SETH BRADFORD (1801–1878), DUDLEY NEWTON (1845–1907). The work of these three architects can be found primarily in Newport and account for the majority of the nineteenth-century structures standing today. While each man had a signature style, collectively their work forms the core of the mid- to late nineteenth-century city we enjoy today (map nos. 6, 7, 8).

ALFRED SMITH (1809–1886) was born in Middletown, Rhode Island, and trained to be a tailor. His vision for Newport prompted his return to the area, where his inspired ideas of the city transformed it into a Victorian picturesque location. Smith developed the Kay-Catherine Street neighborhood, later partnered with Joe Bailey to create the Bellevue Avenue mansion district of the city and completed the transformation with the Ocean Drive that connects Thames Street with Bellevue Avenue by way of Brenton Point. His business acumen included financing sales and renting out the Newport houses of the wealthiest citizens when they were away from the City by the Sea (map no. 9).

Mahlon Van Horne (1840–1910) was pastor of the Union Colored Congregational Church in Newport for twenty-eight years and later served as the U.S. consul to St. Thomas, Danish West Indies. In 1871, Reverend Van Horne became the first person of color to serve on the Newport School Committee and the first to serve in the state's General Assembly in 1885. (map no. 49)

George H. Norman (1827–1900) was a founding member of the *Newport Daily News* in 1846. He became interested in the modernizing of cities and formed companies that built gas and water works in numerous locations. George Norman developed and built the water system that serves Newport today (map no. 50).

Notable Gilded Age Entrepreneurs/Financiers' Burials

August Belmont (1813–1890) was chairman of the Democratic National Committee from 1860 to 1872 and founder of the Belmont Stakes. His marriage to Caroline Slidell Perry connected him to an established Newport family (map no. 10).

August Belmont Jr. (1853–1924) developed the IRT Subway in New York City and the Cape Cod Canal (map no. 11).

Henry Gurdon Marquand (1819–1902) was an American financier, philanthropist and art collector. He was instrumental in establishing the Metropolitan Museum of Art in New York (map no. 47).

Frank K. Sturgis (1847–1932) was president of the New York Stock Exchange (map no. 12).

The Belmont Chapel was designed by George C. Mason for August Belmont as a memorial to Belmont's deceased nineteen-year-old daughter. *Photo by the author.*

Notable U.S. Navy, Army Burials

GLADYS CARR BOLHOUSE (1899–1995) was a U.S. Navy veteran of World War I and local historian (map no. 13).

GUNNER GEORGE F. (or P.) BRADY (1867–1903) earned the Congressional Medal of Honor for his service during the Spanish-American War (map no. 26).

CAPTAIN KIDDER BREEZE (1831–1881) was the commander of the naval landing party at the Second Battle of Fort Fisher in January 1865 (map no. 15).

BREVET BRIGADIER GENERAL HENRY BREWERTON (1801–1879) entered West Point at age twelve, the youngest cadet in West Point history. He later served as superintendent of West Point Military Academy from 1845 to 1852. In addition, he oversaw the construction of many forts, including Fort Adams in Newport from 1827 to 1828 (map no. 16).

REAR ADMIRAL AUGUSTUS CASE (1813–1893) was a career Navy officer who served in the Spanish-American and Civil Wars (map no. 17).

Lieutenant Thomas Eadie, USN (1887–1974) was awarded the Medal of Honor for using his diving skills to rescue a fellow Navy diver (map no. 18, buried in Island Cemetery Annex).

Captain Christopher Raymond Perry (1761–1818) was a privateer in the American Revolution and naval officer in the Quasi-War (map no. 19).

Commodore Matthew C. Perry (1794–1858) commanded the Black Ships Expedition to Japan in 1853, which opened trade with the West (map no. 20).

Commodore Oliver Hazard Perry (1785–1819) was the hero of the Battle of Lake Erie in the War of 1812 (map no. 21).

Major General Thomas W. Sherman (1813–1879) was a Civil War general (map no. 22).

Brevet Brigadier General Hazard Stevens (1842–1918) earned the Medal of Honor for his efforts at Fort Huger in Virginia. He was one of the team that was the first to climb Mount Rainier in 1870 (map no. 23).

Major General Isaac Ingalls Stevens (1818–1862) was a Civil War general killed in action at the Battle of Chantilly. He served as governor for the Territory of Washington from 1853 to 1857 (map no. 23).

Brevet Brigadier General George W. Tew (1829–1884) was a Civil War officer, lieutenant colonel of the Fifth Rhode Island Heavy Artillery and commander of the Artillery Company of Newport (map no. 24).

Commodore Benjamin J. Totten (1806–1877) was a career U.S. Navy officer (map no. 25).

Major General Gouverneur K. Warren (1830–1882) was chief engineer of the Army of the Potomac at the Battle of Gettysburg. As a result of his actions there, he is often referred to as the Hero of Little Big Top (map no. 14).

Newport Mayors

George Henry Calvert (1803–1889), writer and mayor of Newport (map no. 27).

William Cole Cozzens (1811–1876), mayor of Newport and governor of Rhode Island, 1863 (map no. 28).

Lieutenant Colonel John Hare Powel Jr. (1837–1892), Union Army officer, mayor of Newport and commander of the Artillery Company of Newport (map no. 29).

Rhode Island United States Congressmen

PERRY BELMONT (1851–1947), U.S. representative and Army officer (map no. 30).

MELVILLE BULL (1854–1909), U.S. representative, 1895 to 1903 (map no. 31).

HENRY Y. CRANSTON (1789–1864), U.S. representative from Rhode Island and commander of the Artillery Company of Newport (map no. 32).

ROBERT B. CRANSTON (1791–1876), U.S. representative from Rhode Island (map no. 33).

GEORGE GORDON KING (1807–1870), congressman (map no. 34).

GEORGE L. RIVES (1849–1917), U.S. assistant secretary of state (map no. 35).

WILLIAM PAINE SHEFFIELD SR. (1820–1907), congressman and U.S. senator, 1884 to 1885 (map no. 36).

WILLIAM PAINE SHEFFIELD JR. (1857–1919), congressman (map no. 37).

Rhode Island Governors

WILLIAM CHANNING GIBBS (1787–1871), governor of Rhode Island, 1821 to 1824 (map no. 39).

CHARLES C. VAN ZANDT (1830–1894), governor of Rhode Island, 1877 to 1880 (map no. 40).

GEORGE PEABODY WETMORE (1846–1921), governor of Rhode Island and U.S. senator (map no. 41).

Other Notable Burials

KATHERINE PRESCOTT WORMELEY (1830–1908) was a literary translator and founder of the U.S. Sanitary Commission during the Civil War (map no. 38).

GEORGE WASHINGTON GREENE (1811–1883) was an American historian (map no. 42).

CHARLES BIRD KING (1785–1862) was an American portrait painter (map no. 43).

CLARENCE KING (1842–1901) was a geologist and served as the first director of the U.S. Geological Survey (map no. 44).

LEWIS CASS LEDYARD (1851–1932) earned his degree in law and served as president of the New York City Bar Association. He was the personal council to J.P. Morgan and served as commodore of the New York Yacht Club (map no. 45).

Part II

GRAVESTONES AND CARVERS

COLONIAL NEW ENGLAND STONE PRIMER

Tablets, Tables and Boxes

$\mathcal{V}$isitors traveling throughout New England find that the majority of colonial-era gravestones are basically identical. Topped by decorative carved elements in the rounded middle of the stone, each tablet also includes text and possibly side carvings. While stone material varies by location, in Newport, slate was the most commonly used. Most graves were marked with a headstone and a footstone to delineate the location of the body. The carving on the headstone faced west, with the footstone located at the east end of the body. The orientation of the body was intended to allow the person to face the rising sun in the east on Judgment Day. To a lesser

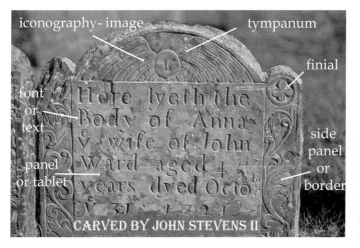

Headstones from the seventeenth and eighteenth centuries were similar in design but display a variety of images (iconography) and information. *Photo by the author.*

Eighteenth-century graves were generally marked with two stones and the body positioned between them. *Photo by the author.*

Bodies were positioned between the headstone and footstone and oriented to face the rising sun on Judgment Day. *Photo by the author.*

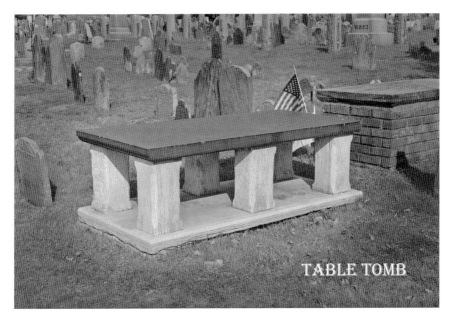

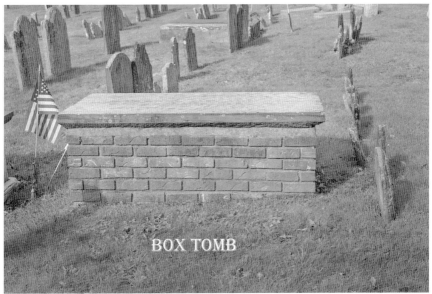

Ledger stones resting on boxes or pillars were costly grave markers. Bodies were buried in the ground. *Photo by the author.*

extent, large horizontal ledger stones were cut and rested on either boxes or pillars. These box or table tombs are not as common as the vertical tablet stones but can be found throughout the city. Regardless of the shape of the monument, bodies were buried in the ground and not in the box or tomb. Being larger and often featuring excessive carving, ledger stones on boxes or pillars are an indication the deceased was wealthy or important.

In New England, the art of crafting gravestones began in the late seventeenth century in the Boston area. As the most important town in New England, Boston was influential in the development of gravestone design in the region.

2

BOSTON CARVERS

Spiral, Mumford, Emmes

Some of the earliest carved stones in Newport include a spiral design across the top of the stone and information for the deceased. These stones date from the 1660s, but there is no information about who carved the stones. The oldest stone in the colony of Rhode Island is in Newport for John Coggeshall, dated 1647 but believed to have been carved in 1684 when his wife, Mary, died. Both stones have similar carvings.

According to Chase and Gabel in *Gravestone Chronicles*, in 1700 the major Boston-area stone carvers included Nathaniel Emmes, whose son Henry Emmes carved some stones for Newport graves, and William Mumford (1641–1718), whose gravestone artistry can be found throughout Newport burial sites. The stones from Mumford are some of the oldest (circa 1690)

Some of the oldest stones are decorated with spiral designs. Coggeshall Burial Ground, Common Burial Ground and Clifton burial site have some stones with this design. This stone for Nicholas Easton was carved in 1676. *Photo by Barbara Austin, RIHC.*

Above: Mumford stones often display death heads and gourds. He also carved other designs. *Photo by the author.*

Left: Henry Emmes carved about sixteen stones in Newport and is buried in the Common Burying Ground. *Photo by Barbara Austin, RIHC.*

and most skillfully executed. Mumford trained Nathaniel Emmes as a carver and married Ruth Copp, whose father owned Copp's Hill Burying Ground in Boston. Mumford's daughter grew up, married and moved to Newport. For these reasons, Mumford was perhaps the most influential early stone carver in Newport and New England in his time. This situation changed in 1705 with the arrival of John Stevens.

3

THE STEVENS FAMILY

JOHN STEVENS I (1645–1736)

John Stevens's early history is not known, but he arrived in Newport in 1705 having wed Marcy Rouse in Little Compton, Rhode Island, in 1701/02.[8] He was fifty years old, recently married and needed to provide for his growing family. Primarily a mason, his early gravestone carvings are more etched than sculpted. Vincent Luti believes that a carver from Boston arrived in Newport in about 1715 and provided training for Stevens and at least one of his sons. The Boston carver remained active in Newport until about 1721, and Stevens's carving noticeably improved. In time, Stevens and his four sons and grandson went on to carve the majority of the slate stones used to mark graves in Newport and establish the Stevens style as one of the best in the country. Their work can be found along the East Coast, and six generations of the family continued the business. In 1724, at age seventy-nine, John retired and the business was placed in the hands of his first son, twenty-two-year-old John Stevens II.

---

8. Little Compton Historical Society, *Remember Me: A Guide to Little Compton's 46 Cemeteries* (Chelsea, MI: Sheridan Books, 2018), 120.

The early work of John Stevens I resembles a muffin with a face. It is more etched than carved and has a flat appearance. *Photo by the author.*

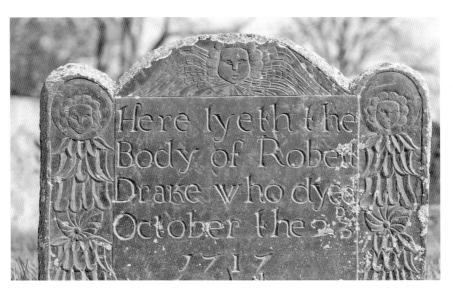

The later work of John Stevens is exhibited on this stone and has a more sculptural quality. *Photo by the author.*

John Stevens II (1702–1778)

John Stevens II, like his father, was primarily a mason. In addition to numerous foundations and fireplaces, he also worked on major buildings, including the Redwood Library and Touro Synagogue. When he became head of the family business, he assumed the responsibility of caring for his parents and younger siblings. In a politically divided city as the Revolution neared, John Stevens II was a Patriot.

As a stone carver, John Stevens II was thirteen to eighteen years old when the Boston teacher was here and was most likely trained to carve by that teacher. His style matured and solidified the Stevens style of carving, which features a front-facing bald soul effigy with wings carved in black flinty slate. John Stevens II bought 29 Thames Street about 1757 but lived and worked at 30 Thames Street, which was also his father's shop and home. It is likely his widowed sister, Martha Bissell, lived at 29 for a time before it became the current Stevens Shop location.

John Stevens II carved many ledger stones that included family crests. *Photo by Barbara Austin, RIHC.*

John Stevens II's carving exemplifies the style that reflects the work of the Stevens family. *Photo by the author.*

30 Thames Street. This was the site for the first three generations of Stevens carvers with the shop in the back of the property. That part of the land was later sold and buildings constructed. *Photo by the author.*

PHILIP STEVENS (1706–1736)

The second son of John Stevens, Philip Stevens had a carving style very much like the Boston teacher who arrived in Newport to teach his father and brothers. While there is no record confirming the idea that he was trained by the Boston carver, the similarities in the work of the two men supports the conclusion. Stones by Philip Stevens are masterfully carved, and his work exhibits a variety of images masterfully rendered. Sadly, his life was cut short when he died in 1736, an event noted in the ledger of his brother John Stevens II, simply stating that Philip Stevens was murdered.

Philip Stevens's work (*stone on the right*) is most like the Boston carver (*stone on the left*) who trained members of the Stevens family. *Photos by Barbara Austin, RIHC.*

James Stevens (1708–1765)

As the third son of John Stevens, James Stevens knew he would not inherit the family business and needed to embark on a different career. Like some of his brothers, James Stevens took to the sea to earn a living and became a merchant sea captain. While on shore he did carve gravestones, but they are not as numerous or as finely done as the work of his three brothers. James Stevens was a founding member of the United Brethren Society in Newport. When he drowned at sea, he willed his possessions to his wife and his younger brother, William Stevens.

William Stevens (1710–1790)

The youngest of the Stevens sons, William Stevens grew up and engaged in a variety of occupations, including seaman, merchant and stone carver. Of all the Stevens carvers, William Stevens is credited with carving the greatest number of stones in Newport. His marriage to Ann Bull resulted in a stormy connection to his brother-in-law John Bull, who became his indentured servant and apprentice and later rival. During the Revolution, William Stevens moved to Philadelphia, where it is believed he died and is buried.

William Stevens's work resembled the work of brother John but used wigs more often on his carved heads. *Photo by Barbara Austin, RIHC.*

His carving style started out similar to his father's and brother John's style but evolved into his own. Wigged effigies, full-bellied "5s" and other carved elements can be used to identify stones by William. His most unique stone element was the incising of eyebrows and eyelashes on faces.

JOHN STEVENS III (1753–1817)

John Stevens III, the grandson of the founder and son of John Stevens II, was the first family member to view himself primarily as an artist. This educated young man was not a mason like his father or grandfather. His early stones resemble his father's style, but John Stevens III later used the side-facing effigy as did John Bull. He also carved images for people of African heritage that are considered to exhibit African facial features rather than the majority of stones that display European features. During his carving career, John Stevens III signed his stones, something the other family members did not do. His signature can be found as J. Stevens, Jun'r or as J. Stevens.

This page, top: John Stevens III was the only family member to carve side-facing effigies. John Bull was another carver who used side-facing images. *Photo by the author.*

This page, bottom: Most signatures for John Stevens III are at the bottom of the stone. *Photo by the author.*

Opposite: This stone was carved by Philip Stevens II. *Photo by the author.*

In memory of
MR. BENJAMIN PITMAN
who died June 9, 1811.
in the 45 Year
of his Age.
And of his Wife
REMEMBER PITMAN,
who died July 28, 1840,
Aged 71.

"Blessed are the dead who die in the Lord
for they rest from their labours.

CARVED BY PHILIP STEVENS II
great-grandson of the founder

John Stevens III's son, Philip Stevens, a fourth-generation carver, and Philip's sons, Lysander and Edwin Stevens, fifth-generation carvers, and Philip Stevens III, a sixth-generation carver, continued the Stevens carving tradition. As styles changed and machine-carved stones entered the business, the work of the later generations is not considered as significant as the work of the family members who preceded them.

4

JOHN BULL

When his older brother mishandled the family finances, John Bull (1734–1808) was contracted to indentured servitude in 1747 to his brother-in-law William Stevens. Stevens trained Bull to be a stone carver. The two men did not get along, and John Bull left Newport for years and earned his living at sea. When he did return to Newport, Bull returned to carving gravestones in a rival shop to his brother-in-law. Stevens sued Bull for breaking his contract, but the court eventually found in Bull's favor.

As a carver, Bull's early work resembled the work of his teacher. As his style matured, he became Newport's most artistic carver. In addition to the typical Stevens images, Bull produced a signature side-facing effigy framed by a scythe and hourglass. He also carved some of the most creative stones in the city, including the Bardin stone with its biblical theme and the Desire

A gaunt effigy framed by scythe and hourglass is praised for its soulful expression. This is John Bull's signature image. *Photo by the author.*

John Bull carved this image, which was either unusual (Moses parting the Red Sea) or blasphemous (depiction of God) for its time. *Photo by the author.*

Tripp stone depicting the deceased's buried arm. As a result of injuries or infections, amputation was fairly common in the 1780s. Religious belief that bodies would be healed on Judgement Day may have encouraged the faithful to bury amputated limbs to be reunited with torsos. Carving the location of the limb on the stone is unusual. The six-humped six-foot-long stone for the deceased Langley children with side-facing effigies (cherubs) is another of his remarkable carvings.

5

POMPE STEVENS

*P*ompe Stevens is another carver with links to William Stevens, as he was enslaved in Stevens's service. This African carver signed two stones in God's Little Acre, and his hand most likely helped create numerous other stones for William Stevens. Other than the signatures on the stones and the link to Stevens, the only other information we know is

William Stevens is believed to be the carver of this stone for the child of Pompe, who was a member of his household. *Photo by the author.*

that Cuffe Gibbs was his brother, which is stated on the stone he carved, and likely had a son, "Princ." Pompe Stevens is the only known African stone carver in Newport, making him one of the earliest artists of African descent in the country.

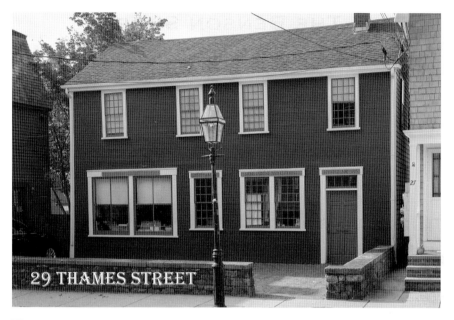

The current location of the Stevens Shop. *Photo by the author*.

6

THE BENSON SHOP

JOHN HOWARD BENSON (1901–1956)

John Howard Benson is buried in the Common Burying Ground.
Photo by Barbara Austin, RIHC.

In 1927, the Stevens Shop and its contents were purchased by John Howard Benson, who revived the hand-chiseled artistry of the Stevens carvers and revitalized the shop. His early lettering, based on the work of John Stevens II but inspired by the work of the Romans, transformed into a unique style. In addition to his exquisite stonework, Benson was also a teacher and author of books about both sculpture and calligraphy. He enjoyed a long teaching career at the Rhode Island School of Design. In 1945, his interest in preserving the Hunter House included a meeting with Katherine and George Warren.[9] That meeting not only saved the house but also contributed to the birth of the Preservation Society of Newport County. Benson was also heavily involved with the restoration of the Governor Arnold Burial Ground in 1946.

9. Jannine Falino, *The Newport Experience: Sustaining Historic Preservation into the 21ˢᵗ Century* (New York: Scala Arts Publishers Inc. and the Preservation Society of Newport County, 2020), 9.

John Everett "Fud" Benson (1939–)

Fud Benson was born in Newport and began working for his father by the age of fifteen. He was a student at the Rhode Island School of Design. In 1964, Benson was commissioned to carve the inscriptions for the John F. Kennedy Memorial at Arlington Cemetery. Today his lettering can be seen on numerous monuments, including the National Art Gallery; Vietnam Veterans Memorial in Washington, D.C.; and the Civil Rights Memorial in Montgomery, Alabama. In 2000, Benson's twenty-five inscriptions on the Franklin Delano Roosevelt Memorial in Washington, D.C., earned him the Presidential Design Award for Excellence in the Arts.

Nick Waite Benson (1964–)

Nick Benson is a third-generation stone carver at the Stevens Shop. After studying drawing, design, calligraphy and typography, he joined his father in the shop in 1988, and in 1993 took charge of the business. Under Nick Benson's direction, the shop has lettered many national sites, including the National World War II Memorial, National Gallery of Art and the Martin Luther King Jr. Memorial in Washington. From university buildings to gravestones, his font based on classic Greek letters greets thousands of people each day. He was honored in 2007 with the National Heritage Fellowship Award and in 2010 named a MacArthur Fellow, awarded to people who have shown "extraordinary originality and dedication in their creative pursuits and a marked capacity for self-direction."

GRAVESTONE CARVERS IN COLONIAL NEWPORT, RHODE ISLAND

NAME (BIRTH-DEATH)	ACTIVE CARVING YEARS	STYLE	COMMENTS
Boston master (teacher)	1715–1721	winged skulls	trained John Stevens I and perhaps a son or two
William Mumford (1641–1718)	1685–1700	winged skulls, winged effigies, highly sculptural at an early time in Newport	trained Nathaniel Emmes, father of Henry Emmes; married to Ruth Copp, Copp's Burial Ground in Boston
John Stevens I (1645–September 18, 1736)	1705–1724	1705–1715: skulls, incomplete lower jaw (fringed teeth); incomplete 5; dotted "i"; wings attached but straight out; finial spoke wheel or stylized rose; gouged not sculpted; capital letters until 1713, starts lowercase letters; 1715–1724: more sculptural, from death heads to effigies	built house and shop at 30 Thames 1709, enlarged circa 1750; was a mason and a stone cutter
John Stevens II (February 22, 1702–April 17, 1778)	1719–1778	"e" is centered over "y" in "ye"; 5 not complete; used few wigs, more like caps; did not use cupid bow mouth	took over business in 1724 and cared for the Stevens family; mason and carver; bought lot at 29 Thames; built house sometime between 1757 and 1848; Zingo was an enslaved bricklayer

Name (Birth-Death)	Active Carving Years	Style	Comments
Philip Stevens I (1706–April 6, 1736*) *date in John II account book)	1721–1735	bulb skull square-shaped; work resembles the Boston carvers; big "O" in "of"	went to sea; was murdered; stones in his style end 1735
James Stevens (1708–August 4, 1765)	1729–1734	cruder than other Stevens stones	merchant sea captain; among founders of the United Brethren Society in Newport; drowned at sea; willed possessions to wife and brother William
William Stevens (September 7, 1710–1784 or 90)	1727–1775 Leaves Newport for Philadelphia	William "e" is to the right top of the "y"; full-bellied 5; eye lash etched eyes; uses wigs; uses cupid's bow mouth	in 1742 married Ann Bull; Mariner; in 1736 moved out of 30 Thames, bought 9 Cross Street; in 1747 moved merchant business to Long Wharf; leading stone carver in Newport in output; enslaved African Pompe who signed two stones
John Stevens III (March 1753/54–1817)	1769–c.1800	only Stevens to use cherub; used three-quarter view; carved all stones exhibiting African features	only Stevens to sign work; signed as J. Stevens or J. Stevens, Junior (until 1778); educated as an artist, not laborer

Name (birth-death)	Active carving years	Style	Comments
Phillip Stevens II (January 9, 1793– September 13, 1875)	c.1810–1875		youngest son of John III (fourth generation); bought 34 Thames Street in 1816; carved in back shed; in 1848 took over shop from brothers
Lysander Stevens (August 7, 1821– May 22, 1895)	c.1840–1895		son of Philip II (fifth generation); brother of Edwin
Edwin Stevens (1833–1900)		sculptor of marble	last Stevens owner of 30 Thames Street; son of Philip II; left shop to brother-in-law who leased space until Benson purchased in 1927
John Bull (September 8, 1734–November 28, 1808)	1747–1798 Blind last ten years of life	"e" to the right of "y"; cupid's bow mouth often; scythe and hourglass—not all stones; full or gaunt face; uses three-quarter view	in 1747 indentured to brother-in-law William Stevens; in 1768 lawsuit initiated by William Stevens; cherub image used with simpler borders later in life
Henry Emmes (1716–1767)	1763–1767	portraits, skulls	oldest son of carver Nathaniel Emmes; related to William Codner, a noted carver

Principal Carvers in Colonial Newport and Years of Most Active Work

1700	1710	1720	1730	1740	17
	John Stevens I 1705–1724				
			John Stevens II 1719–1778		
			William Stevens 1727–1775		
		Philip Stevens I 1721–1735			
			James Stevens 1729–1734		
					John Bull ▶
Boston master 1715–1721 William Mumford 1685– 1700					

The Stevens Stonecutters (bolded)

founder	**John I**			
son	**John II**	**William**	**James**	**Philipx**
grandson	**John III**			
great-grandson	**Philip II** (1793–1875)	William	James	John IVx
2x great-grandson	**Lysander** (1822–1895) marble worker	**Edwin** (1833–1900)		
3x great-grandson	**Philip III (1850-1917)** marble cutter; carves 1868-1876;			

1760	1770	1780	1790	1800

John Stevens III 1769–1810

3

Philip Stevens II

Henry Emmes 1763–1767

Stone tidbits

Old carved Ss looks like an F in some uses; relic is a widow; in 1753/54, colonies switched from Julian calendar to Gregorian calendar; newer wording is "In memory of."

Part III

PRESERVATION AND DOCUMENTATION

1

EARLY RECORDS

Gravestones and grave sites captured the interest of Newport from the early days of the city. Many times, family histories, including deaths, were recorded in family Bibles and in the documents of religious congregations. Perhaps the first known exploration of the Common Burying Ground was by Reverend John Comer in the 1720s.[10] Comer was the fifth minister (1725–1731) for the congregation started by Dr. John Clarke. A more significant documentation of the Common Burying Ground was done by Dr. Ezra Stiles, minister to Newport's Second Congregational Church and librarian at the Redwood Library. Stiles copied gravestone inscriptions and recorded deaths in his "Bills of Mortality," 1760–1776. Additional sources of death information include the records of the Society of Friends (Quakers) as well as account books, diaries, probate records and newspaper articles

Family and church death records continued after the Revolution, and the evolution of the funeral business and the role of undertakers in death-related matters provided additional sources of information. The Newport Historical Society, established in 1854, became a significant source for documenting Newport burials early in its existence. George H. Richardson completed a transcript of the graves by 1875 for the society, and Dr. Henry E. Turner's work was completed in the 1890s. Documents from both men are included in the society archives.

---

10. Sterling, *Newport, Rhode Island Colonial Burial Grounds*, 3.

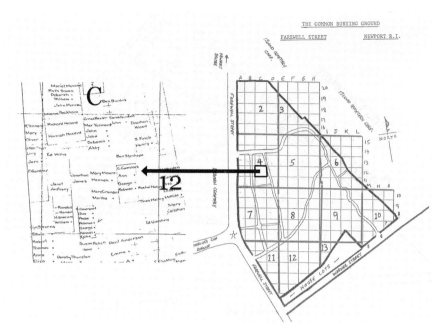

The 1903 map was divided into sections and names of the deceased recorded. A small section is reproduced on the left. *Photo by the author.*

In June 1903, the city authorized the first inclusive documentation of burials in the Common Burying Ground. A map was created indicating the location of each stone by name. A grid was imposed over the site, creating 345 squares in which burials were recorded. The index to the site identified the names of the buried person and their square coordinates. This document is an essential guide for anyone looking for a gravestone today, as it shows not only the stone's location but also places it among its neighboring stones. Since the site evolved in a disorganized pattern, this tool is invaluable for locating stones. While useful, the 1903 map is challenging to use.

At the time of the American Bicentennial (1975–76), Edwin Connelly, director of Rhode Island Cemeteries, undertook a project to document and restore burial grounds in Newport. With a grant from the Comprehensive Employment and Training Act and the assistance of volunteers, including members of the Naval War College History Club, stones in the Common Burying Ground were transcribed, detailed drawings of the stones created and data recorded. In 1977, the group completed a map and an updated index of the Common Burying Ground.

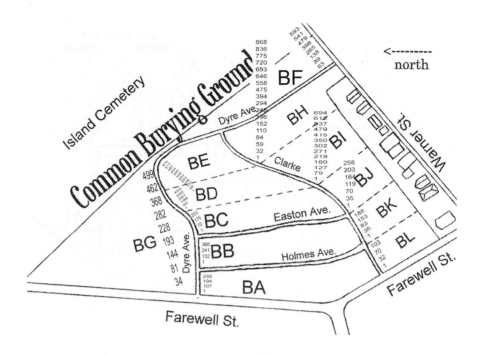

The numbers added to the Beaman map show each row in a section. For example, in Section "BA," row 1 would be graves 1–106, and grave 107 would be the first grave in row 2 on the left. *Photo by the author.*

In 1982–83 Alden G. Beaman redesigned the Common Burying Ground map and replaced the earlier grid designation with two-letter section labels that incorporated the existing roads on site. Location numbers within each section for each stone were later added (2006–9) by John Sterling and his team, and this is the database currently used for the site.

2

GRAVE SITE AND GRAVESTONE

CHAMPIONS

*A*s with any form of historic preservation, there is a need to inventory what exists and its condition before planning for its preservation, and gravestone preservation is no different. The documents from Comer, Stiles and the others were the foundation for any efforts to preserve stones and sites and should be considered the first preservation efforts. Known preservation of Newport's historic stones and sites began in earnest in the 1970s in large part through the efforts of Edwin Connelly.

Edwin Wilmot Connelly (1927–2001) was the first director of the Veterans Memorial Cemetery in Exeter, Rhode Island, established in 1974. He documented more than two thousand historic burial grounds in Rhode Island for the state's Department of Veterans Affairs. As the first state cemeteries director, he was proud of his work with the Rhode Island Veterans Cemetery and oversaw the completion of the chapel at the veterans' site and several war memorial monuments.[11] At that time, Connelly was also actively involved in Newport documenting graves in the Common Burying Ground. In 1974, the Common Burying Ground and the Island Cemetery were added to the National Register of Historic Places. Not surprisingly, the majority of the photographs submitted with the application were captured by Edwin Connelly. Under his direction, about forty unearthed slate gravestones were stored at the Rhode Island Veterans Cemetery or the Coggeshall Burying site awaiting repair and return to their proper places.

---

11. "Obituaries," *Providence Journal*, July 6, 2001, C0-4.

A reprint of an article from the *Providence Journal* sometime in the 1970s. From the *Providence Journal*.

In 1992, the stones in Exeter were rediscovered by John Sterling, who assisted Ron Onorato, John Canham and James Garman in returning them to Newport. About this time, a number of additional stones were discovered in use as a patio in Portsmouth, Rhode Island. Onorato and Canham were able to obtain the return of these stones. Conditions were not right to reset the stones from each location, so John Canham was able to store them at Swiss Village Farm until the team was ready. For a time, some stones went to the Great Friends Meeting House and some to the John Stevens shop. Onorato engaged students from the University of Rhode Island to help identify the original location for many of the stones, and installation was completed in 1996. Some of the stones remained with Professor Onorato's collection at the University of Rhode Island and were used with students. Stones from the collection were relocated to appropriate sites in 2021 by the Newport Historic Cemetery Advisory Commission with Onorato's participation. Documentation of the location of each stone moved from the university can be found in the records of the commission. Additionally, in October 2018, six stones that had been stored in the Coggeshall burial site in Newport by Connelly in the 1970s were returned to ground in the Common Burying Ground.

The importance of the work of John Sterling, Barbara J. Austin and Letty R. Champion in Newport between 2006 and 2009 cannot be overemphasized. Sterling directed the effort to document every gravestone in all Newport colonial grave sites. The effort was based on numerous data sources, and a high-quality photograph of every stone was produced. The publication of *Newport, Rhode Island Colonial Burial Grounds, Special Publication No. 10* by the Rhode Island Genealogical Society in 2009 was the culmination of three hundred years of data documenting these historic sites. In addition to the published document, the information was added to a website (rihistoriccemeteries.org), providing a modern tool for researchers of Rhode Island history and genealogy.

3

HISTORIC CEMETERY
ADVISORY COMMISSION

*W*hile some grave sites are owned by individuals or congregations, the City of Newport is the responsible organization for numerous sites, the largest being the Common Burying Ground. In 1993, the Common Burying Ground Commission was established to "develop a comprehensive planning strategy to preserve, restore and manage the site." The commission established guidelines for mowing, inventorying stones and some resetting of stones. By 2004, city funds for resetting stones had been cut to fund mowing of the site. The commission was restructured in 2006 as the Historic Cemetery Advisory Commission but went dormant after May 16, 2007. In the fall of 2015, concerns were raised about deteriorating slate stones and activity in the Common Burying Ground. Every known interested organization or individual was invited to attend a meeting held on January 29, 2016, at the Newport Public Library to discuss the concerns. Represented were the City of Newport, the Preservation Society of Newport County, the Newport Historical Society, the Rhode Island Historic Cemetery Commission, the Rhode Island Genealogical Society, the Newport Restoration Foundation, the 1696 Heritage Group and Salve Regina University. While many ideas were discussed at this and subsequent meetings, the revival of the cemetery commission was deemed the most important action to take. With the guidance of city councilor Lynn Ceglie and the support of city council, the commission was revived at the March 23, 2016 Newport City Council meeting and new members sworn in June 8, 2016.

This logo was created in 2017 by Lakuna Graphic Designs with direction from the Historic Cemetery Advisory Commission. *City of Newport.*

Since that time, the commission has worked with the city to promote, preserve and protect historic burials sites. Guidelines have been adopted for stonework, new signage added to the Common Burying Ground, gravestones cleaned, tours and programs presented to the public and scholarship encouraged. The most important accomplishment has been the treatment of more than 270 gravestones and the cleaning of hundreds of additional stones. The first work for the Duchess and Violet Quamino stones was done by Dr. Robert Russell, a local gravestone preservation practitioner who had done previous work for the city. The following year, with the commission's participation, the city hired Beyond the Gravestone to undertake all gravestone work in Newport. With limited funding to treat deteriorating stones, the commission decided to concentrate on a limited section of the Common Burying Ground so the completed work would have the most impact. The selected section, known as God's Little Acre, contained more than one hundred slate stones in danger of losing historic integrity if not soon treated. The section's importance as the largest collection in the country of professionally carved stones for eighteenth-century people of African heritage made this the logical place to start work.

Treatment of slate stones is the most expensive and least noticeable of the stonework. With this in mind, the commission decided to divide city funds to treat not only slate stones but also marble and granite to improve the overall appearance of the site. The cost for granite and marble work is lower than slate and the effect on the site is more visible than slate work. City funding allowed about six slate stones to be treated each year, so

The most important rule of gravestone work is to do no damage to the existing material. These marble stones, shown before and after treatment, were restored using proper epoxies and mortar. *Photo by Lisa Cornell.*

it would take sixteen years to secure the future of these important slate stones. Even with private donations, the work would take at least ten years to treat the slate stones needing work just in this one section. With the assistance of the Preservation Society of Newport County, a $50,000 grant was awarded in 2019 for the treatment of forty slate stones from the African American Cultural Heritage Action Fund of the National Trust for Historic Preservation. Additional funds from a private donor were obtained, and ten additional stones were treated in 2020 with a commitment to treat the remaining stones in 2021. If all goes as planned, all identified slate stones needing treatment in God's Little Acre will have

The decision to add as little material as possible to seal stone edges resulted in the removal of some new material (*pictured top right*) from this stone. The final repair (*bottom right*), like any stonework, should be reversible. *Photo by Lisa Cornell.*

been treated by the end of 2021. Securing the future of these historic artifacts is a significant achievement.

The commission determined that not all gravestones were worthy of treatment. New England weather has reduced many slate stones to fragments of their original condition. Stones without significant visible details on the stone face will not be treated. They will simply continue to weather and their particles return to the ground. Marble stones that have fallen and fractured into numerous parts can only be restored with the use of metal frames and appropriate epoxies. The aesthetic of the frames as well as the costs to treat each of these monuments led the commission to decline work on these

Slate gravestones located in the Common Burying Ground. *Photo by the author.*

stones. The aesthetics of the site and the stones was also a consideration in deciding how to treat slate stones that had missing portions but maintained important features. The commission decided to seal the edges of the stone and add a minimal amount of new material. Preserving the historic material on these stones without additions to re-create the original stone shape was the accepted action taken.

In 2020, a general survey of the Common Burying Ground was made to estimate the amount of stonework needed. A conservative estimate is that at least 450 stones and 25 box tombs need to be treated. This work will cost a minimum of $562,000, and costs will only increase if treatment is delayed. With numerous burial sites to maintain, the city and the commission will have work to do for many years to come.

Additional gravestone work by individuals and organizations other than the city has also taken place. Island Cemetery, the Colonial Jewish Burial Ground, St. Joseph's Cemetery, Trinity Church and the Arnold Burial site have had gravestones treated and burials documented. Newport has been a place with strong interest in historic preservation for more than a century, and that interest extends to our many burial sites.

APPENDIX

COMPLETE LIST OF BURIAL SITES
IN NEWPORT, RHODE ISLAND

he source of the information in this table is found on the state
database and taken verbatim from that source.
http://rihistoriccemeteries.org/newsearchcemetery.aspx.

NT001   ISLAND CEMETERY

The "History of Newport County, Rhode Island," ed. Richard M. Bayles,
NY, 1888 contains the following description of Island Cemetery: The town
of Newport, on the 18th of May, 1836, purchased a tract of land, which
was the beginning of the cemetery now known as the "Island Cemetery," on
Warner street. Early the next year Mr. Henry Bull and William W. Freeborn
were appointed to lay out the new burial ground. In 1839 a certain portion
was surveyed and laid out into one hundred and thirty-six lots, each one rod
square. These were offered for sale at moderate rates. In 1844 the balance
of the purchase was laid out, avenues made, trees and shrubbery set out,
and a substantial fence built, the wall and the gateway costing $831.33. In
1848 a company was formed to whom the town conveyed the grounds. The
trustees of the "Island Cemetery Company" were authorized to take care
of the property, to grant deeds of lots unsold and to adopt the necessary
means for raising funds as might be required for the purposes of the new
company. Several additions have been made to the original purchase, thus
affording better conveniences, and rendering this spot a fitting repository
for the dead. Recently a fine freestone chapel has been built by the

Honorable August Belmont, near the lot owned by him, wherein rest the remains of Commodore M.C. Perry. The grounds are tastefully laid out and contain many beautiful lots, where the hand of affection has been lavish in its adornments, and loving hearts have reared elaborate and expensive monuments" (p. 543). Many of the earlier inscriptions were recorded by Dr. Henry E. Turner, who was involved in an official capacity (secretary of Willow Cemetery) with the cemetery. This manuscript is at the Newport Historical Society; typed transcriptions of it, unfortunately made after it had significantly deteriorated, are there and at the Rhode Island Historical Society. Turner's records have been entered and are coded HET. From the mid-1980's through the early 1990's Alden G. Beaman published a selective record of transcriptions in the Rhode Island Genealogical Register. He chose to record almost exclusively couples born before 1850, thus creating an excellent reference for marriages, but leaving out single people and children. Beaman noted platform stones, group monuments, hedges, and otherwise fenced plots. Individual stones are mentioned only if the condition interferes with reading the inscription. His data has been entered and is coded AGB. In January 1996 John Sterling visited Virginia Sampson who will mark her 70th anniversary working at the cemetery next year. When the Island Cemetery was incorporated in 1848, two cemeteries (New Burying Ground, 1840 and Willow Cemetery, 1852) were located on the grounds. Original lot deeds are in the safe. She says the cemetery has records for 11,409 interments, many on cards made in the 1920's by a previous superintendent. As of April 1996, we have 3,378 names from Island and another 165 from Willow for a total of 3,543 from this cemetery. It will be noted that quite a few of the names predate the official founding of the cemetery, perhaps moved by descendants to this more elegant burial ground or perhaps erected before the cemetery was incorporated. The boundary of the cemetery is as follows: 41 deg. 29' 43.40"N x 71 deg. 18' 49.74"W on Warner St. 41 deg. 29' 50.22"N x 71 deg. 19' 00.65"W on Farewell St. 41 deg. 29' 55.21"N x 71 deg. 19' 01.06"W on Van Zandt Ave. 41 deg. 29' 57.42"N x 71 deg. 18' 50.28"W on Van Zandt at Vicksburg Pl. 41 deg. 29' 45.66"N x 71 deg. 18' 46.45"W on Warner St.

NT002   ISLAND ANNEX CEMETERY

purchased August 11, 1926 from Arend Brandt (city records). Although there are supposedly 300 burials, only two (NORTH husband and wife who died in the 1930's) met Beaman's criterion of birth before 1850 and thus are entered in the database. This is the modern section.

NT003 COMMON BURIAL GROUND

A land grant to Newport by Dr. John Clarke, 1640. Bayles' "History of Newport County," NY, 1888, describes it thus: "The "Common Ground," so called, is the oldest public cemetery in Newport. It was laid out about 1665. It remains today in all its primitive surroundings, and the quaint headstones of common slate, with their rude inscriptions, awaken a feeling of veneration which surrounds this spot with no little degree of interest. Here may be seen the graves of many of the early governors of the colony, that of a signer of the Declaration of Independence, the graves of our early merchants and clerical worthies. Many stones are dedicated the memory of old sea captains. The cemetery contains twenty stones on which armorial ensigns are cut; all of these lie flat on the surface of the ground while most were originally box tombs, and of course have, like most of the early stones in this ground, suffered every sort of injury, even in a few cases, mutilation. Among the stones on which family arms are cut may be mentioned the Cranstons, Sanford, Bayley, Wanton, Thurston, Chaloner, Buckmaster, Freebody, Vernon, Ellery, Sears, Gardner and Ward. One might almost write a history of Newport in this common ground, so full are the inscriptions on the stones erected here" (pp. 542-543).

NT004 BRAMAN CEMETERY

This cemetery is also called Rhode Island Historical Cemetery Newport #4. It is located on Fairwell (sic) Street opposite the Common Burial Ground. Only husband and wife pairs born through 1850 were recorded by Beamon until 2020, when the entire site was documented. It was active during most of the twentieth century and includes Jewish sections, sections for U.S. Navy related burials, and reflects the diversity of the city. The cemetery was established in 1898 by David Braman, Daniel Braman, and Robert Fell on land that had been part of the family farm. It was active during most of the twentieth century and includes Jewish sections, sections for U.S. Navy related burials, and reflects the diversity of the city. In 1981 the site was forfeited to the City of Newport which currently maintains the site. The original site plans and plot sale records are located in City Hall. Naval burials- Newport has had a connection to the U.S. Navy since Colonial times. A "new" Navy hospital opened in 1910 and was expanded in 1918 to accommodate 1000 patients. In addition to graves for people who served in the military living or retired in Newport, the cemetery also has two sections purchased by the hospital for those who died there. Greek burials- By 1896 four Greeks were known to have been in Newport from the island of Skiathos and would be soon joined by others from Skiathos and Lesbos. Opportunities in the local fishing industry and tensions between Greece and Turkey may have encouraged people to move to Newport. The growing Greek community would be employed in a variety of jobs in the city in addition to the fishing industry. Saint Spyridon congregation was chartered in 1915 and worshipped many places before buying their current house of worship on Thames street in 1924. Jewish sections-Newport's Congregation Jeshuat Israel (CJI) established a cemetery fund in October of 1895 but didn't immediately act to purchase land. In the meantime, a group of Newport Jews, not all of whom were affiliated with the congregation, formed the Goel Zedeick Society and purchased six lots in the City-owned North Common Burying Ground. This is the small fenced area located near the northwest corner of Van Zandt Avenue and Farewell Street. There were only 3 internments there, the last one taking place in 1944. The death of Mrs. Florence Engell in November of 1898 moved CJI to use the previously established burial fund to purchase 10 lots in the privately-owned Braman Cemetery, located on Farewell Street south of the North Common Burying Ground; two additional lots were purchased between 1899 and 1905. These comprise the present Section III. The granite and limestone entrance gates were dedicated in 1911. At least two people, a Dannin daughter and grandson, were reinterred in Section III from unspecified unconsecrated ground. Four more lots were purchased by the congregation sometime later in what became Section II. Another portion of Section II consists of 20 lots south of the CJI section purchased and resold between 1906 and 1935 by a number of individuals and organizations, many of whom were not affiliated with Touro Synagogue. Separate areas were owned by CJI, the Cheva Kadisha (a burial society established circa 1913), B'rith Abraham Lodge No. 294, and B'rith Shalom Lodge No. 255. Section I consists of 8 lots purchased between 1925 and 1927 with some plots being resold into the 1930s. Most of the people buried here were members of Newport's Congregation Ahavas Achim, but the lots were purchased by individuals or families, not by the congregation. All of these various burials were brought together under the oversight of the newly chartered Jewish Cemetery Unification Association in 1976. The gravestones in this cemetery were photographed in 2020 by Lew Keen.

NT005   OLD CITY CEMETERY (NORTH CEME)

Alden Beaman notes: "This cemetery is also called City Cemetery and Rhode Island Historical Cemetery Newport #5. It is located on Fairwell (sic) Street opposite the Common Burial Ground. It is a fairly modern cemetery…" Beaman recorded only husband-wife pairs born through 1850 and not children since they had no children and therefor were not of interest to genealogists, acording to him. This cemetery was photographed in 2019 and 2020 by Lew Keen.

NT006   ST MARY'S CEMETERY

This church was built in the early 1850's when the congregation outgrew the previous Catholic church, St. Joseph's on Barney St. Victorian transcribers and descriptive writers appear to have ignored the cemetery. Robert Hayman's "Catholicism in Rhode Island" mentions the church in passing, gives further reference to the history privately printed in 1902: "Golden Jubilee of the Church of the Holy Name of Mary, Our Lady of the Isle, Newport, R.I., 1852-1902." The inscriptions were selectively transcribed by Alden G. Beaman (AGB) and published in the "RI Genealogical Register," 8:343-352 and 9:81-86. As usual he copied only husband-wife pairs born before 1850, with the addition of some widows whose husbands are named. When this cemetery ran out of room in the 1890s the church started using Columbia's Roman Catholic Cemetery in Middletown (MT004) to bury its parishioners.

NT007   JOHN CLARKE BURIAL GROUND

History of Newport County, Rhode Island," New York, 1888, ed. Richard M. Bayles: "On West Broadway is a little cemetery containing the graves of Dr. John Clarke, one of the founders of Newport and pastor of the First Baptist church. He died in 1676. Here also rest the remains of Reverend John Callender and other pastors of this church. Calender died in 1748." This cemetery is in beautiful condition: walled on one side, with an iron fence on a stone base, and padlocked iron gate. The standard RI Historical Cemetery sign is not in evidence, but there is an elegant sign with the following inscription: JOHN CLARKE CEMETERY To the memory of Dr. John Clarke, 1609-1676 Clergyman Physician Statesman Leader of the settlers who purchased Aquidneck Island from the Indians on March 24 1638. He was the first pastor of the church now known as The Un. Baptist Church John Clarke Memorial, located at 30 Spring St. As agent for the Rhode Island Colony in England for twelve years from 1651, John Clarke procured the Charter of 1663 from King Charles II, which secured "full liberty in religious concernments." A permanent trust created in his will dated April 20 1696 continues to provide income "for the relief of the poor or the bringing up of children unto learning." Inscriptions were transcribed by Alden Beaman (AGB) and published in "Rhode Island Genealogical Register." GPS coordinates 41 deg 29' 37.68"N x 71 deg. 18' 40.58"N

NT008   FRIENDS BURIAL GROUND

A refreshing open space in a very built-up neighborhood, the cemetery is surrounded by a chain-link fence. The sign is so badly rusted that it can hardly be read; it is propped up against the fence. Clearly many of the stones have disappeared as there are wide grassy patches. Presumably many of the people noted in Quaker records are actually buried here---but we may never know because the stones have gone or were, in the early Quaker way, never inscribed. Some of the names in the database come from Alden Beaman's transcription (AGB), some from the continuing efforts of Len Panaggio (LP). In 2006 Barb Austin and Letty Champion photographed all of the stones in this cemetery. These photographs were then used to correct the transcript in the database and to add over 100 stones not transcribed previously. A note in Quaker records for Jacob Mott who died in 1779 at age 88 (perhaps in Newport, perhaps not) gives an interesting glimpse of the past of this cemetery. It says that he was buried in his own ground, "the meeting house and yard [this cemetery] occupied by Hessians." GPS coordinates 41 deg. 29' 36.74"N x 71 deg. 18' 49.42"W

NT009   CODDINGTON BURIAL GROUND

On Farewell Street just south of N. Baptist St. Recorded 14 Aug 1869 by G.H. Richardson (GHR) "all the legible inscriptions in the Coddington Burying Ground, CETA volunteers in the 1970's, and also by Alden G. Beaman (AGB) in the 1980's. "History of Newport County, Rhode Island," New York, 1888, ed. Richard M. Bayles, notes: "On Farewll street, near the First Baptist church, is the Coddington ground. Here are the graves of Governors Henry Bull. Who died in 1693; Nicholas Easton, 1675; John Easton, 1705; and William Coddington, 1678---four of the original settlers of Newport. In this ground are buried many of the first inhabitants." A nice photograph of this cemetery appears in "The Architectural Heritage of Newport, Rhode Island," showing the walls and relationship to adjoining houses. The photo is captioned "Cemetery of Governors." There is an 1873 transcript of this lot by William John Potts of Camden, NJ at NEHGS that calls this the Old Graveyard of the North Baptist Church. GPS coordinates (WGS84 datum) 41 deg. 29' 32.91"N x 71 deg. 18' 51.79"W

NT010   TRINITY CHURCH YARD

History of Newport County, Rhode Island," New York, 1888, ed. Richard M. Bayles: "The ancient burial place connected with Trinity church, on Church street, is an object of much interest. Several of the early pastors of the church lie buried here. Here may be found the ground of the French Admiral de Ternay, who died in 1780, and of many others who fought in the war of the revolution. On eight stones are found the arms of five families: Gidley, Wanton, Bell, Goulding, Gibbs, representing a few of the wealthy merchants of Newport in the last century." When Bayles wrote the description above, the cemetery had already been given a full chapter in George Champlin Mason's "Reminiscences of Newport," 1884, with good, early information on the gravestones (GCM). Mason provides many names that have since disappeared; his account is rich in biographical detail. The inscriptions were recorded again about 1900 by Jonas Bergner (1859-1936) in a beautiful ms at Redwood Library in Newport "Ye Grave Stones in Trinity Church Yard." This book contains complete transcriptions of the inscriptions, very careful pen and ink drawings of armorial carvings, some light pencil sketches of stones, and names of carvers when known. Although only the most cursory comparison has yet been made, names only from Bergner are coded JB. CETA volunteers drew stones & inscriptions in the late 1970s on cards in the possession of Edward W. Connelly, director of the project. These have been used to confirm or amplify inscriptions recorded summer of 1995 by John Sterling with help of passing tourists! These names are input with the code JES. For further information on those buried here, consult James N. Arnold's "Trinity Church Newport, Deaths and Burials," 10:537-544. It is worth noting that only a small percentage of members of the church are actually buried in this medium-sized lot. To illustrate this point, consider Ezra Stiles' record of some 188 deaths of Episcopalians during 1760 through 1764; of 39 remaining gravestones only four are here, most of the others at the Common Burial Ground (NT003). Earliest burial Thomas Fox 1707. GPS coordinates 41 deg. 29' 14.75"N x 71 deg. 18' 47.57"W

NT011   GOV. BENEDICT ARNOLD GRAVEYARD

Although this cemetery is extremely important from both the historical and artistic perspectives, it was literally buried for many years and only saved by the most dedicated, backbreaking work. See Alice Brayton's book "The Burying Place of Governor Arnold," Newport, RI, 1960 for the story of its restoration and fine photographs of the excellent carvings and inscriptions. Most stones have an individual photograph and biographical sketch of the person for whom it was carved. The material has been entered in the database and is coded JB (John Howard Benson). An undated, but surely late 19th century transcript by George Henry Richardson (GHR) has preserved readings of many now lost stones in their original location. These are noted "GHR only, not found 1960." Richardson's ms can be seen at Newport Historical Society. Those interested in even greater details of the cemetery at the turn of the twentieth century should consult the "Report of J.N. Arnold, Commissioner to inquire into the present condition of the Governor Benedict Arnold Burial Place, and the title thereto, made to the General Assembly at its January Session, 1901," Providence, 1901. This pamphlet contains a wealth of historical detail and three maps, as well as two different transcriptions: (1) two stones copied in 1858 by Dr. Henry Jackson (HJ) and (2) seven stones copied by an anonymous friend of Arnold's (ANON). In addition to the original burials, there are graves moved into the cemetery in living memory. An undocumented note in our database for MT020, the Weeden Lot formerly at Green End & Valley Rd., Middletown, says that John Howard Benson, then owner of the Arnold graveyard and the Stevens shop, had the graves moved in 1960. The note does not specify the number, but it likely was small, as Richardson recorded only two in the Middletown cemetery in the late 19th century. GPS coordinates 41 deg. 29' 09.56"N x 71 deg. 18' 43.25"W

NT012   UNITED CONGREGATIONAL CHURCHYARD

This cemetery contains the graves of two Congregational ministers, one of which (1839) was removed at a so-far unknown date from an older cemetery attached to the First Congregational church on Mill St. The second, a monument, commemorates a pastor of the 2nd Congregational church, who died in Hartford CT. in 1839 (Hon. Robert Franklin, "Newport Cemeteries," Special Bulletin #10 of NHS, Dec. 1913, pp. 44-45). GPS coordinates 41 deg. 29' 08.57"N x 71 deg. 18' 46.27"W

NT013   COLONIAL JEWISH BURYING GROUND

First Jewish burial ground in RI. The Hebrew congregation was formed in 1658 in Newport. George Champlin Mason's "Reminscences of Newport," Newport, 1884, states that "In the City Clerk's office there is a copy of a deed, dated Feb. 28, 1677, of a lot of land bought by Mordecai Capanall and Moses Pacheckoe, for a burial place for Jews, which lot was enlarged by later purchases" (p.69). The "History of Newport County," ed. Henry Bayles, NY, 1888, describes it in some detail: "This beautiful spot is well known to the many thousands who visit Newport. It is situated on Kay and Touro streets, surrounded by a granite wall and iron fence, with a plain square gateway, over which is cut in bold relief a winged globe. This cemetery of the ancient Hebrew congregation was acquired in the year 1677. Here are buried many of the early members of this congregation. The inscriptions on the stones are in Hebrew, Latin, Portuguese, Spanish and English. When the Hebrew congregation was broken up, in consequence of the removal of its members to other cities, the burial ground was suffered to fall into neglect and decay. In 1820 Mr. Abraham Touro, then a resident of Boston, visited Newport and gave directions for the erection of a brick wall, which for many years afforded ample protection to the cemetery. In 1842 his brother Judah Touro, a resident of New Orleans, caused the grounds to be put in perfect order, and replaced the brick wall with the present substantial fence. At his death he bequeathed a considerable sum in trust to the city of Newport for the perpetual care of this cemetery. The trust is faithfully and well discharged" (p. 544). Henry Wadsworth Longfellow mentions this beneficence in his poem "The Jewish Cemetery at Newport": "Gone are the living, but the dead remain, / And not neglected for a hand unseen, / Scattering its bounty, like a summer rain, / Still keeps their graves and their remembrance green" (Putnams' Magazine, June 1854, p. 81). In his lecture later published as a special bulletin of the Newport Historical Society, the Hon. Robert Franklin discusses this cemetery and quotes extensively from an address given before the society in 1885 by Rev. A.P. Mendes. Mendes had pointed out that all inscriptions began or ended with the phrase "May his soul be bound in the bands of life," that the word "died" is never used, that the Hebrew inscription contains only the dates and age, whereas the English one can be lengthy and flowery. While ordinarily in Jewish cemeteries the date of death is expressed in a chronogram formed on some verse of scripture, Mendes found only one example here, that of Abraham Touro's stone. See the Hon. Robert Franklin, "Newport Cemeteries," Special Bulletin of the Newport Historical Society, #10, pp.30-32. Touro Cemetery may long have been a landmark in Newport, but its multilingual inscriptions appear to have daunted past transcribers. The 40 names entered into the database were collected by (1) the Rev. Abraham Pereira Mendes (APM) in 1875 for his paper "The Jewish Cemetery" read before the Newport Historical Society and (2) Morris A. Gutstein (MAG) for an appendix to his book "The Story of the Jews of Newport," NY, 1936, pp. 295-321. Gutstein's book is particularly valuable. He provides a map of the cemetery, discusses anomalies in the burials and possibilities of graves having been moved or built upon. His numbering system has been used in our database. GPS coordinates 41 deg. 29' 16.53"N x 71 deg. 18' 33.62"W

NT014   CLIFTON BURIAL GROUND

Called Clifton Burial Ground after the first owner of the land, Thomas Clifton, who left it in his will in 1675 to the Society of Friends. It is also known as Golden Hill Burial Ground, named for the street it is located on. An index card at Newport Historical Society points out that some stones predate the will. Many Quakers are buried here, but in general the stones are elaborately rather than severely carved. Many notable citizens of early Newport, including FREEBORN CLARKE, a daughter of Roger Williams, and her second husband GOV. WALTER CLARKE rest here. The Governors Wanton are buried here. The Hon. Robert S. Franklin asserted in his 1911/1912 speech "Newport Cemeteries" that the family vault of Gov. Joseph Wanton was built at the expense of Joseph & William Wanton in 1771. He quoted, possibly from a now missing inscription, that bodies of the wife and son of Joseph Wanton, Sr. and the wife and children of Joseph Wanton, Jr. were moved to the vault Oct. 18, 1771. Other bones of the Wanton family were dug up, some from the Common Ground, some from Bristol. (See the reprint in SPECIAL BULLETIN of the Newport Historical Society, No. Ten, Newport, RI, Dec. 1910). A 1996 cursory examination revealed only a raised mound with only two WANTON names. See also "Three Hundred Years of the Governors of Rhode Island," pp. 135-137. Beside the many historically interesting persons buried here, this cemetery is notable for an exceptionally fine collection of gravestones concentrated in a small area. The Stevens family of stone carvers is well represented; one also finds many Bull and Mumford stones. As of March 1996, the cemetery was clean, neatly trimmed, with few broken or down stones, a tribute to recent efforts by neighbors and the Newport Parks Commission. In 1869 H.T. Tuckerman described a different picture: "Rank weeds have overgrown the pathless little enclosure, over which the poor dwellers of the neighborhood spread their washed garments to bleach" ("The Graves of Newport," Harpers' Magazine, Aug. 1869). A hundred years later in 1969 it was still described as in poor condition. Numerous sources document burials in this lot, beginning with the Friends' Record published in Arnold (QUAK) which provides many names for which no stones exist now and likely never did. George Henry Richardson (GHR) transcribed the lot in 1873 (document at

Newport Historical Society). Benjamin F. Wilbour and Waldo C. Sprague (WS) recorded inscriptions in natural order in 1956 (document at NEHGS in Boston). CETA volunteers in the mid-1970s sketched gravestones in natural order. Alden G. Beaman (AGB) published his transcription of "all stones which could be read" in his Rhode Island Genealogical Register," vol. 11, 1988, pp. 309-314. Most recently John E. Sterling (JES) read the gravestones in late 1997 for phase 2 of the RI Historic Cemetery Project and Barb Austin and Letty Champion photographed every gravestone in 2007. Note that many gravestones in this cemetery have dates given in Quaker format where the month is given Called Clifton Burial Ground after the first owner of the land, Thomas Clifton, who left it in his will in 1675 to the Society of Friends. It is also known as Golden Hill Burial Ground, named for the street it is located on. An index card at Newport Historical Society points out that some stones predate the will. Many Quakers are buried here, but in general the stones are elaborately rather than severely carved. Many notable citizens of early Newport, including FREEBORN CLARKE, a daughter of Roger Williams, and her second husband GOV. WALTER CLARKE rest here. The Governors Wanton are buried here. The Hon. Robert S. Franklin asserted in his 1911/1912 speech "Newport Cemeteries" that the family vault of Gov. Joseph Wanton was built at the expense of Joseph & William Wanton in 1771. He quoted, possibly from a now missing inscription, that bodies of the wife and son of Joseph Wanton, Sr. and the wife and children of Joseph Wanton, Jr. were moved to the vault Oct. 18, 1771. Other bones of the Wanton family were dug up, some from the Common Ground, some from Bristol. (See the reprint in SPECIAL BULLETIN of the Newport Historical Society, No. Ten, Newport, RI, Dec. 1910). A 1996 cursory examination revealed only a raised mound with only two WANTON names. See also "Three Hundred Years of the Governors of Rhode Island," pp. 135-137. Beside the many historically interesting persons buried here, this cemetery is notable for an exceptionally fine collection of gravestones concentrated in a small area. The Stevens family of stone carvers is well represented; one also finds many Bull and Mumford stones. As of March 1996, the cemetery was clean, neatly trimmed, with few broken or down stones, a tribute to recent efforts by neighbors and the Newport Parks Commission. In 1869 H.T. Tuckerman described a different picture: "Rank weeds have overgrown the pathless little enclosure, over which the poor dwellers of the neighborhood spread their washed garments to bleach" ("The Graves of Newport," Harpers' Magazine, Aug. 1869). A hundred years later in 1969 it was still described as in poor condition. Numerous sources document burials in this lot, beginning with the Friends' Record published in Arnold (QUAK) which provides many names for which no stones exist now and likely never did. George Henry Richardson (GHR) transcribed the lot in 1873 (ms at Newport Historical Society). Benjamin F. Wilbour and Waldo C. Sprague (WS) recorded inscriptions in natural order in 1956 (ms at NEHGS in Boston). CETA volunteers in the mid-1970s sketched gravestones in natural order. Alden G. Beaman (AGB) published his transcription of "all stones which could be read" in his Rhode Island Genealogical Register," vol. 11, 1988, pp. 309-314. Most recently John E. Sterling (JES) read the gravestones in late 1997 for phase 2 of the RI Historic Cemetery Project and Barb Austin and Letty Champion photographed every gravestone in 2007. Note that many gravestones in this cemetery have dates given in Quaker format where the month is given as a number. Before 1752 the Julian calendar was in use and the first month was March. The dates from the gravestones have been converted to the Gregorian calendar now in use.

NT015   JONATHAN EASTON BURIAL GROUND

History of Newport County, Rhode Island," New York, 1888, ed. Richard M. Bayles, mentions this lot as being "in good order." Robert Franklin mentions it as "a small walled enclosure, originally part of the old Easton farm, containing the graves of members of the Easton family" ("Newport Cemeteries," SPECIAL BULLETIN of the Newport Historical Society, Newport, RI, 1913, p. 43). Transcriptions by Alden Beaman published in "Rhode Island Genealogical Register," vol. 10. GPS coordinates 41 deg. 28' 53.18"N x 71 deg. 18' 0.10"W

NT016   COGGESHALL BURIAL GROUND

History of Newport County, Rhode Island," New York, 1888, ed. Richard M. Bayles: "On Coggeshall Avenue is a little burial ground of about one acre, [actually 0.11 acre] inclosed by a handsome stone wall, with an iron gate in the central front, over which is chiselled "COGGESHALL, 1854." The interior is kept in perfect order, the stones free from stain. In the center is a granite obelisk bearing the following inscription: "To the memory of John Coggeshall, First president of the Colony, died Nov. 27, 1647, Aet. 57." The original stone bearing the same inscription is still preserved at the head of the grave." Transcribed by George H. Richardson (GHR) on 19 Aug. 1869, by CETA volunteers in the 1970's, and Alden Beaman (AGB) in the 1980's. GPS coordinates 41 deg. 28' 07.25"N x 71 deg. 18' 35.52"W

NT017   FORT ADAMS CEMETERY

Margaret Beaman's note with 8 transcriptions: "This is a military cemetery with the graves in meticulously straight rows which are widely separated. It is in a field (park) near the Ocean (Narragansett Bay) and fenced with a neat hedge. The older graves are nearer the Ocean. The last 2-4 rows furthest removed from the Ocean are of persons who died in the 1930's and 1940's. Many of the stones give only a death date with no birth date or age at death. In a few rows from the most recent graves are those who died in World War I and the 1920's. Most persons in the military cemetery died young; it is probably for this reason that we found no husband and wife both buried together in this cemetery." (1991) Her transcriptions are coded MB. In 1995 John Sterling transcribed all the stones and input the data under the code JES. GPS coordinates 41 deg. 28' 21.55"N x 71 deg. 20' 40.77"W

NT018   COLLINS BURIAL GROUND

Small cemetery for members of the COLLINS family, including JOHN COLLINS, Governor of Rhode Island 1786-1790. A monument says the stones were restored and protected by Dr. John G. Warren of Boston and Andrew Collins of Louisiana in 1854. Transcribed by G.H. Richardson (GHR) in the Victorian period and by John Sterling (JES) in 1992.

NT019   ST. JOSEPH'S OLD CATHOLIC CEMETERY

Although currently linked with St. Mary's Catholic church, this cemetery was originally set out for St. Joseph's, the first Catholic church in Rhode Island, which was formed in 1828. Its stones commemorate early Irish immigrants, most of them in the prime of life, giving their original town and county in Ireland. The church grew to become St. Mary's, and the first building (a former schoolhouse) was sold. The "Newport Mercury" for Feb. 27, 1864 says: "Workmen are at present busy in stripping off the boards and taking up the floor, previous to its removal, of the old Catholic Church on Mt. Vernon St. It was sold at auction to Mr. Michael Butler in Perry St.,who intends using the boards in the erection of small tenements, a class of house now much needed" (index card at NHS). The marble stones were laid down many years ago. The Museum of Newport Irish History restored the cemetery in 1999, restored and up-righted the gravestones, and installed an informational plaque on the Barney Street side of the lot. Bertram Lippincott III published transcriptions and a brief history of the church in "Rhode Island Roots," Dec. 1990, pp. 109-111).

NT020   JUDGE ANTHONY WILBUR LOT

Richard M. Bayles describes the "Wilbor burial place on Bliss Road" as being "in good order" (History of Newport County, Rhode Island, 1888). At the end of Wilbur Ave. running south from Bliss Rd. south of #6 Wilbur Ave. In 2001 Len DeAngelis has adopted this cemetery and has started to restore it. See Newport Daily News Sect B, p. 1, Wednesday, August 22, 2001. It is next to #6 Wilbur Ave. GPS coordinates 41 deg. 29' 51.32" x 71 deg. 18' 7.44" (WGS84 datum) - map in little yellow notebook.

NT022   SABBATARIAN CHURCH CEMETERY

The now-extinct Sabbatarian Church in Newport flourished between Dec. 23, 1671 and 1836, with its greatest period of membership and prosperity before the Revolution. See Arnold, 7:623-634 and 11: 297-307 for records. Church building now belongs to the Newport Historical Society. Only 1 burial, that of Elder William Bliss, is supposed to be from the cemetery; the stone now leans against a wall at NHS. 8 other members, including a pastor and a deacon, are buried at the Common Burial Ground, one is at the Island Cemetery. Unclear whether the church actually had its own cemetery. In 2006 there are 3 stones here. Samuel Hubbard and his wife, Tase Cooper, formed the first Seventh Day Baptist Church in America in 1671. They were buried in Middletown Historical Cemetery #59 at Berkley's Whitehall Farm. Ezra Stiles recorded his gravestone in 1763. This burial ground was taken up and some of the stones placed into the stone wall. Those that survive are now in the basement of the Middletown Historical Society. Some members of the Sabbatarian Church fled Newport during the British occupation during the Revolutionary War and took refuge in Hopkinton, site of a Sabbatarian Church. Mary Tanner "of Newport" is buried in their burial ground which is now in the First Hopkinton Cemetery (HP022). Her stone reads "...who to escape the storms and dangers of an unnatural and cruel civil war, took refuge in a rural retreat..."

NT023   MARLBORO ST TOMB

Governor Jeremiah Clarke was buried in a tomb at the foot of Marlboro St. This cemetery no longer exists

NT024   COASTER'S HARBOR SMALL POX BG

The burial ground was originally located at the location where there is now a tennis court. The gravestones were placed on the ground on a hillside on the south side of Hopkins Ave. Information on missing stones is from G.H. Richardson transcript of 1870, and from a manuscript at the Newport Historical Society titled "List and Location of gravestones in cemetery C. H. I." It was sent to the Society in 1917 by Commander R. Z. Johnson. Each gravestone has a dimension in the burial ground that reads like "4 ft. west side of cemetery, 15 ft. from south side." With these dimensions we can determine that the burial ground was 125 ft. by 50 ft. and contained six rows of gravestones. Coaster's Harbor is where the Naval War College is located. Transcribed and entered by John Sterling (JES). GPS coordinates (WGS84 datum) 41 deg. 30' 28.25N x 71 deg. 19' 37.05"W for the location of the gravestone on the hillside.

NT025   G. E. MORAVIAN CHURCH LOT

This branch of the Moravian or United Brethren sect was founded in Newport in 1749, records begin Nov. of 1758. A house of worship was built in 1767-1768 on the site of the present Kay Chapel (built in 1869). Henry Turner notes that Mary Malling (1712-1772) gave the lot from which her remains were removed; Arnold cites the deed from Mary Mallens to Society of United Brethren in Bk. 16, Land Evidence, p.53 (Arnold, 7:610). Arnold's transcription of the church records (ibid.) gives names of 84 members who died between late Nov. 1758 and Mar. 1833. It is not known whether all of these were originally buried in the Moravian lot, but certainly some were. Tuckerman mentions this former cemetery in his article "The Graves of Newport" in Harpers' Magazine, Aug. 1869: "Thus, in the Schoolhouse Yard, on Church Street, two or three upright grave-stones hidden amidst bushes and weeds mark the site of the Moravian church, since converted into an Episcopal chapel--the sect having died out in the place" (p. 373). The "Newport Mercury" for Nov. 11, 1882 has an article "THE MORAVIAN CHURCH-The Disposition of the Remains from the Old Burying Ground." On information received from John H. Greene, the writer states that at the time the property was sold, the remains were removed by James A. Greene and Samuel Engs to the Common Burial Ground. In the family lot of John and Samuel I. Greene a white marble monument commemorated Richard, Thomas, and Mary Hayward, as well as Mary Malling; it says that the remains were moved in July 1867. Of the 84 names we have records of 24 stones in our database, all but 1 in the Common Burial Ground. The other is in the Willow section of the Island cemetery.

NT026   GARDE LOT

Writing of the Common Burial Ground, the Hon. Robert Franklin says: "Among the oldest stones in this cemetery are those placed over the tombs of John Garde and his wife. They were originally buried on their estate on the west side of Thames street, near what is now known as Champlin's wharf, but some time before the year 1800 they were removed to the common burial ground" ("Newport Cemeteries," Special Bulletin of the Newport Historical Society, #10, Newport, 1913, p.7). It's not clear whether any other people were buried there, and if so, whether their graves were moved or ever transcribed. The stones still exist at the Common Burial Ground, although Mrs. Garde's appears to have been repaired or recast.

NT027   GOV. CALEB CARR GROUND

Was located on Mill Street west of the Coddington School. Removed to Jamestown in 1900. Now registered as JM001 & NT027 to indicate it original location and the present location. Mentioned in G.H. Richardson's "Scrapbook," Book 974, p. 24, print of ms at NHS. Richardson says the bodies were removed to Jamestown by a descendant (Mrs. John Foster Carr) Sept. 8, 1900 and reburied at a site on the west side of East South Road. See transit permit dated 10 September 1900 in the Jamestown Town Clerk's office.

NT028   DIXON BURIAL PLACE

Recorded by G H Richardson 19 Aug 1869. Despite the name of the cemetery, the surviving inscriptions all are for TAYLOR family members (with the exception of PATIENCE PECKHAM), mostly buried between 1757 and 1766. This lot appears to have been moved to Island Cemetery (NT001) as Turner places stones which Richardson placed here in Island instead (for example, SARAH (TAYLOR) WILLIAMS, BENJAMIN TAYLOR, and PATIENCE PECKHAM). The "History of Newport County" does not mention it in 1888, so presumably the graves were moved between Richardson's visit in 1869 and that date.

NT029   DYRE FAMILY BURIAL GROUND

Recorded by G H Richardson 1870. He gives the exact location as "Dyre's Farm, late Robert L. Maitlands" (GH Richardson Scrapbook 974, Vol. A, copy at NHS). Staff at NHS believe this property was located roughly where the Naval Hospital was built opposite Coaster's Island. Richardson describes the moving of the graves as a consequence of development: "These stones were removed to the _____ Wm. lot in Old Ground [Common Burial Ground] Oct. 25, 1889, the farm then being cut up into house lots and the burial ground left in the street."

NT030   PELEG WOOD LOT
recorded by George Richardson in 1870 at the corner of Freebody and Broad St. It has been removed to the Common Burying Ground (NT003) section BH.

NT031   FIRST CONGREGATIONAL CHURCHYARD
was on Mill St. Graves moved to NT012

NT032   GOAT ISLAND BURIAL GROUND
We only know about this burial ground by the ledger stone for Samuel Carr and his daughter that is leaning against the side wall of the Newport Historical Society and by the George Richardson transcript of 1894. He notes: "North end of torpedo station - Goat Island … the father and daughter died of small pox which was quite prevalent at Newport at this time (1739)."

NT033   JAHLEEL BRENTON BURIAL GROUND
This burial ground is next to the Fort Adams Cemetery. The only gravestone there now is that of Jaleel Brenton, son of the Governor. When William Brenton came to New England, he carried with him a commission from King Charles I that allowed him to choose a 2000-acre tract of land in Newport that is now called Brenton Point. This is the location of Fort Adams and Governor Brenton's farm called Hammersmith. Governor Brenton's box tomb is no longer there but we have a pretty good description of its purchase by his son Jaleel in the John Stevens account book: Mr. Jaleel Brenton 1727 L S P one double tomb stone for the Governor 45 - 00 - 00 600 bricks at 6 shillings a hundred 01 - 16 - 00 lime 11 bushels 00 - 13 - 09 sand bushels @ 6 a bushel 00 - 04 - 00 two stones for the foundation 00 - 08 - 00 carting the bricks and lime and sand 00 - 07 - 00 carting the tomb stone 01 - 00 - 00 cutting the coat of arms 05 - 10 - 00 building ye boxes 02 - 10 - 00 _____ 57 - 08 - 09 According to the dates this tombstone was built 53 years after the death of Governor William Brenton. We have never found a recording of it in place so it probably disappeared before 1875 when Richardson was recording the burial grounds in Newport. GPS coordinates (WGS84 datum) 41 deg. 28' 21.24"N x 71 deg. 20' 42.82"W

NT034   GRAVES POINT LOT

Two stones, one with an inscription, recorded by G.H. Richardson in his scrapbook (Book 794, p. 46, print of microfilm at NHS). H.T. Tuckerman in his article "The Graves at Newport" (Harpers' Magazine, Aug. 1869, p. 372) refers to the graves of shipwrecked sailors near Brenton reef. Richardson's transcription is in fact for a 15-year-old who was drowned, whether from a ship or not is not stated. The 1888 edition of G.M. Hopkins' "City Atlas of Newport, Rhode Island," printed in Philadelphia, shows two rectangles marked "graves 1772" on Graves Point between Ocean Avenue (now Ocean Drive) and the sea. Richardson's sketch shows them on the other---the land---side of the road. As they have long since been washed away, the matter is academic. Temporary cemetery number was NT505.

NT500   WILLOW CEMETERY

When Island Cemetery was incorporated in 1848, there were two cemeteries situated on the grounds: the "New Burying Ground" and Willow Cemetery. The original lot deed for Willow Cemetery, signed by Henry E. Turner, is dated2 Jan. 1852; it is in the safe at Island Cemetery. Four file drawers there contain cards of lot maps and names, made by a previous superintendent in the 1920's. Although Dr. Turner lists transcriptions of stones in Willow Cemetery separately in his collection, other transcribers do not make a distinction, and Willow no longer has an identity as a separate cemetery.

NT503   BLISS-PIERCE LOT

Recorded by G H Richardson in his Scrapbook 974, vol. A, copy at Newport Historical Society. On his first visit (say 1870) he gave the location as "rear of Felix Peckham's, at corner of Everett St. at Broadway. He revisited the lot 27 May 1918 and gave the location as "at rear of Loresta." This area is completely covered with houses today.

NT504   DANIEL GOOLD LOT

Location unknown today. See *Newport Mercury* Saturday January 30, 1864. "in removing the Fairbanks house from its location on Bowery Street, a gravestone was found with the following inscription legibly cut upon it. "Here lieth the body of Ruth the daughter of Major Nathaniel Sheffield and Mary his wife and wife of Daniel Gould who died March ye 16th 1712 in the 21st year of her age."

NT600   NEWPORT LOCATION UNKNOWN

Not a cemetery. These names come from Quaker death records rather than from inscriptions on stones; they are in the database as a temporary aid to researchers. Presumably individuals are buried in several cemeteries, many of these are marked by plain fieldstones according to Quaker tradition and some may have never had stones. Where stones have been identified, names have been placed in the appropriate cemetery. Records were transcribed by John Sterling.

NT602   JOHN TAYLOR'S FARM

One known burial, that of ALICE LEE, 2nd, from Quaker records. Significantly she died during the period during which the Hessians were occupying the Quaker meeting house and burial ground, and had to be buried in a private rather than communal site. Town not known to be Newport with certainty. Location unknown

NT604   JACOB MOTT'S BURIAL GROUND

He was buried "in his own ground" in 1778 because the Quaker meeting house and yard were occupied by Hessians. Unknown whether there were any other burials, unlikely that any stone exists today. Town might have been Portsmouth where many MOTTs lived. Location unknown

NT605   ROBERT TAYLER'S ORCHARD

Single burial (ROBERT TAYLER, 1653-1707) from Quaker records. Possibly in Newport. Location unknown

BIBLIOGRAPHY

Bacon, Allison. "The John Stevens House at 30 Thames Street, Newport, Rhode Island." Roger Williams University, December 6, 2016. http://rwu.academia.edu/AllisonBacon.

Baugher, Sherene, and Richard Veit. *The Archeology of American Cemeteries and Grave Markers*. Tallahassee: University Press of Florida, 2014.

Brayton, Alice. *The Burying Place of Governor Arnold*. Newport, RI: Published by the author, 1960.

Burgess, Frederick. *English Churchyard Memorials*. Cambridge, UK: Lutterworth Press, 1963.

Chase, Theodore, and Laura Gabel. *Gravestone Chronicles*. Boston: New England Historic Genealogical Society, 1990.

Falino, Jeannine. *The Newport Experience: Sustaining Historic Preservation into the 21st Century*. New York: Scala Arts Publishers and the Preservation Society of Newport County, 2020.

Forbes, Harriette Merrifield. *Gravestones of Early New England and the Men Who Made Them*. Princeton, NJ: Pyne Press, 1927.

Giguere, Joy. *Characteristically American: Memorial Architecture, National Identity, and the Egyptian Revival*. Knoxville: University of Tennessee Press, 2014.

God's Little Acre. http://www.Colonialcemetery.com/.

Hattendorf, John B. *Semper Eadem: A History of Trinity Church in Newport 1690–2000*. Newport, RI: Trinity Church, 2001.

Historic Ipswich. "Colonial New England Funerals." http://www.historicipswich.org/2019/10/2/colonial-new-england-funerals.

Knoblock, Glenn. *African American Historic Burial Grounds and Gravesites of New England*. Jefferson, NC: McFarland and Company Inc., 2016.

Little Compton Historical Society. *Remember Me: A Guide to Little Compton's 46 Cemeteries*. Chelsea, MI: Sheridan Books, 2018.

Ludwig, Allan I. *Graven Images: New England Stone Carving and Its Symbols, 1650–1815*. Middletown, CT: Wesleyan University Press, 1966.

Luti, Vincent. *Mallet and Chisel*. Boston, MA: New England Historic Genealogical Society, 2002.

Meyer, Richard E. *Cemeteries and Grave Markers: Voices of American Culture*. Logan: Utah State University Press, 1992.

Providence Journal. "Obituaries." July 6, 2001, C0-4.

Rhode Island Historic Cemetery Commission database of graves- http:// rihistoriccemeteries.org/searchgravesnameonly.aspx

Seeman, Erik R. *Death in the New World*. Philadelphia: University of Pennsylvania Press, 2010.

Sterling, John E., et al. *Newport, Rhode Island Colonial Burial Grounds*. Hope: Rhode Island Genealogical Society, Special Publication No. 10, 2009.

Stinson, Brian. Newport Notables." Redwood Library & Athenaeum. 2004. Http://www.redwoodlibrary.org/research-projects/newport-notables.

Strangstad, Lynette. *A Graveyard Preservation Primer*. Plymouth, UK: Altamira Press, 2013.

Tashjian, Dickran, and Ann Tashjian. *Memorials for Children of Change: The Art of Early New England Stonecarving*. Middletown, CT: Wesleyan University Press, 1974.

Youngken, Richard. *African Americans in Newport*. Newport, RI: Newport Historical Society, 1998.

INDEX

Perry, Oliver 70
Powel, John 70

Q

Quakers 52, 53, 105
Quamino 35, 112

R

Redwood 42, 52, 84, 105
Rice, Harriet 37
Rives, George 71

S

Senter, Isaac 28
Sheffield, William 71
Sherman, Thomas 70
Smith, Alfred 67
Spiratos, Nikolas 62
Sterling, John 24, 55, 107, 109
Stevens 82, 95, 97, 109
Stevens, Hazard 70
Stevens, Isaac 70
Stevens, James 86
Stevens, John 12, 37, 42, 81
Stevens, John I 82
Stevens, John II 84, 95
Stevens, John III 31, 87
Stevens, Philip 85
Stevens, Philip II 90
Stevens, Philip III 90
Stevens, Pompe 33, 93, 94, 98
Stevens, William 33, 86, 91, 93
Stuart, Jane 37
Sturgis, Frank 68
Sundquist, Axel 62

T

Tew, George 70
Turner, Henry 105

V

Van Horne, Mahlon 68
van Zandt, Charles 71
Vernon 37

W

Warren, Gouverneur 70
Wetmore, George P 71
Wormeley, Katherine 72

ABOUT THE AUTHOR

*L*ew Keen is a former teacher who shared information in a concise, clear, interesting format for decades. In recent years, these skills have been honed as a tour guide in Newport, Rhode Island, presenting the history of the city to visitors and residents. An interest in burial sites began in the 1980s after visiting Laurel Hill Cemetery in Philadelphia. With an avid interest in all things related to the nineteenth century, cemetery visits to Victorian cemeteries were part of any travel plans. A fascination with Newport's history exposed the need for action to preserve historic gravestones. Lew led the effort in 2016 that resulted in the renewal of the city's Historic Cemetery Advisory Commission. Since that time, he has served as the chair of the commission and later that year was appointed to the state Historical Cemetery Commission.